Maureen Mullally is a practising barriste[r] family law for twenty years. She is a me........ ..... Family Law Bar Association and was recently appointed part-time Chairman of a Child Support Appeal Tribunal. She has seven children, seven grandchildren, and lives in Bickley, Kent with her husband.

LAW AND THE FAMILY

A Practical Guide

Maureen Mullally LL.B.

Hodder & Stoughton
LONDON SYDNEY AUCKLAND

10 9 8 7 6 5 4 3 2 1

British Library Cataloguing in Publication Data

Mullally, Maureen
Law and the Family: Practical Guide
I. Title
344.10615

ISBN 0 340 60793 9

Typeset by Hewer Text Composition Services, Edinburgh
Printed and bound in Great Britain by Mackays of Chatham plc

Hodder and Stoughton Ltd,
A division of Hodder Headline PLC
338 Euston Road
London NW1 3BH

To my dear John who shares my
family and encourages my law

Author's note

All the case studies in this book are completely fictional. They illustrate what might happen in certain circumstances and they have been deliberately simplified. Real life cases are usually infinitely more complicated – and no two cases have identical facts! So please do not compare the facts of your case with any of mine in the belief that it will tell you *exactly* what result you can expect.

Acknowledgments

I would like to acknowledge the help, advice and encouragement which I have had from so many friends and colleagues and in particular Dame Margaret Booth, who inspired in me during my pupillage her own enthusiasm for family law; Angela Hodes who has patiently read the manuscript and made constructive comments; Nora and Mary Rose Mullally, my daughters, who provided the solicitor's view; Tony Bushell, who was always prepared to listen and advise; and Inspector Shirley Tulloch. Last but by no means least, I have to thank Martin, Gary, Samantha and Dave, my Clerks, without whose forbearance the book would never have been finished, and Dawn Bates, who has given such invaluable editorial guidance.

Contents

Foreword

by Helena Kennedy QC

Maureen Mullally's book is that joyful experience: a book about the law which is accessible, informative and easy to read. It penetrates some of the dark recesses of the legal system, which can seem so unfathomable to the very people whom the law is supposed to serve.

Knowing about the law and being able to use it should be the entitlement of every citizen in Britain but, unfortunately, we still shroud the law in too much mystique, with lawyers often using language which excludes understanding and confuses rather than clarifies.

However, the general public is now better informed generally and more demanding of its professionals than ever before. People are no longer prepared to accept the paternalism of the past, which meant being patted on the back and told to leave their case to the experts. They want to be involved in a collaborative process and to embark on any legal journey with a clear understanding of what is involved. Without knowledge how can we make the most important decisions of our lives?

One of the great challenges to any legal system is that it keeps in tune with the changing world. The twentieth century has seen considerable changes in the status of women, which has inevitably led to a renegotiation of relationships between the sexes. People's expectations of marriage are now different and divorce has greatly increased. Childrearing methods have developed, with a greater appreciation of children's needs and a growing emphasis on children's rights and parental responsibility. This period is undoubtedly one of transition with painful consequences for many couples and it is to the courts that they invariably turn for resolution of conflict.

Ready access to the law is a fundamental right in any democracy but it can be meaningless if the process is prohibitively costly and the procedure frighteningly obscure. The battle for wider legal aid provision will have to be confronted in other ways but informative guides like this can provide much-needed knowledge to the non-lawyer.

Families, albeit in greater variety than in previous generations, remain a fundamental part of our social arrangements, crucial to our individual and national wellbeing, often determining who we are and how we relate to the world. They can be a source of stability and nurturance, havens of security and love, but not always. Misty-eyed portrayals of the good, old fashioned family often deny the reality with which the courts have to deal. As Maureen Mullally so lucidly explains, abuses formerly veiled in secrecy, such as incest and domestic violence, are now being openly disclosed. Solutions to such profound social problems cannot rest entirely with the courts but the law has a powerful role in issuing messages which reverberate throughout society.

I know that *Law and the Family* will be an invaluable resource for anyone embarking upon a case in the family courts or anyone wanting a general understanding of family law. The author is a fine lawyer who illuminates her subject with humanity and compassion. For me this book is testimony that light can be shone on the law to the benefit of us all.

Helena Kennedy QC
1994

INTRODUCTION

Why This Book?

Every day of the week, in family courts in every town and county, men, women and children come face to face with the law. You are probably reading this book because the law is affecting or is going to affect you and your family in some way soon. Perhaps your marriage has broken down, maybe you can't decide which one of you the children will live with, or you are trapped in a violent relationship. Whatever your reason for coming into contact with the law, it will no doubt be an emotional and stressful time, a time when the last thing you want to contemplate is being involved in legal proceedings.

To many people the law can seem very intimidating and the mental image which people have of courts and lawyers is no help. TV and film scenes leave viewers with the impression that court proceedings are conducted in an atmosphere of high drama, with witnesses being unmercifully and sarcastically bullied by ruthless and overbearing cross examination. My own husband has always refused to come to see me in court. He says that he has one idea of me and does not want it changed!

The legal jargon alone might leave you feeling completely baffled. You might get into court to find judges and barristers, wigged and gowned like creatures from some other world, speaking what sounds to you like pure gobbledegook, while you are thinking, "Hang on a minute, please. Use words that I can understand. After all, this is *my* life you're talking about."

Well, the good news is that things are not quite like that in family courts. In the first place, it is very unlikely that you will see wigs and gowns. Most cases which have to do with the family are heard in courts which are not open to the public. No one can come into court who is not directly concerned with the case. The judges and other lawyers do not wear their wigs and gowns when the court is closed to the public. There will be a sign outside the court which says "Court in Chambers", and that simply means "Keep out unless this is *your* case".

What Has Happened to Family Law?

Over the past twenty years or so there has been a dramatic change in family law. In our grandparents' day family life was an intensely private business. Marriages, births and deaths had to be registered. Apart from that, unless a crime had been committed, the law left the family strictly alone.

For countless generations, the "family" meant the husband and wife living together until one of them died, bringing up their children, sticking to one another through good times and bad. Nobody moved too far away from where they were born. So brothers and sisters of the partners, grandparents, uncles, aunts and cousins would all be part of normal family life, with everyone supporting each other in their own marriages. Until fairly recently it was unusual for a man and a woman to live together as husband and wife, having a sexual relationship and bringing up children, without going through a ceremony of marriage. Single parent families were only likely to occur when one partner had been widowed. The shame attached to the idea of illegitimacy meant that unmarried mothers were usually forced to give up their babies.

But changes in the structure of the family have meant that the law has had to become more involved in family matters. Many young people leave their home area to work or study at considerable distances away. They marry or start relationships and make new homes far from their families. Cut off from family support by distance, couples tend to find themselves a bit isolated in times of difficulty or trouble. This is a factor which has played its part in increasing the breakdown of relationships and led to a greater acceptance of divorce and single-parenting.

Over recent years there have been many laws passed which deal with the family and there has been a totally new approach to family law. The aim has been to get rid of formality and bewildering legal language as far as humanly possible. Family lawyers, whether they are judges, barristers or solicitors, are keen to make sure that people know exactly what is going on and how what is going on is likely to affect them. Even the Lord Chancellor has invited anyone who may be interested to comment on his suggestions of ways in which the law of divorce might be improved.

How This Book Will Help You

If you are not legally qualified you may find it difficult to know how to set about things when it comes to a legal matter which affects you or your family. For example, what is the first step? Where can you go for advice? Can the law actually help you with your family problem? When you come to court, what can you expect? In the book you will find explanations of many of the most common ways in which law can affect the family on a day-to-day basis, together with suggestions about how you might want to proceed or people you might want to contact. At the end of some chapters there is a list of addresses which may be useful. This is not a legal textbook and I have tried to avoid legal language as far as I can. But it is obviously not always possible to avoid using legal terms and you are bound to come across unfamiliar words. So at the end of the book you will find a glossary of legal terms, giving simple explanations of what they mean. The book is divided into five sections so that you can quickly find the topic you may be looking for.

Scottish Law

Scotland has its own laws, and its family and divorce laws and procedures are not the same as those for England and Wales. However, the Child Support law covers Scotland as well as England and Wales. Citizens Advice Scotland and the Scottish Council of Voluntary Organisations have published a guide to separation and divorce in Scotland, called *Splitting Up*. It is by David Nichols and costs £4.95.

I

Couples

1

ARE YOU SPLITTING UP?

What Used to Happen

In 1936 Edward VIII, already the King of England, was faced with an impossible choice. He had fallen deeply in love with Wallis Simpson. She was an American, which would have been quite bad enough. But even worse was the fact that she had been divorced. The King desperately hoped that he would be able to marry her and, at the same time, keep his crown. But it was made quite clear to him by his advisers that he could not possibly have both the kingship and the woman he loved. This was in spite of his great popularity with the people. However popular he was, it was simply not possible for him to marry someone who had been divorced. He made his choice, and gave up his throne in favour of his brother, the father of Queen Elizabeth II. Edward VIII became the Duke of Windsor, married Wallis, and lived in exile from his own country for the rest of his life. Sometimes it seems hard to believe that all this happened less than sixty years ago.

In the early 1950s Princess Margaret, sister of Queen Elizabeth, fell in love with Group Captain Townsend. He was in many ways a suitable match for a princess, having had a distinguished wartime service career, followed by a stint serving as one of Buckingham Palace's most trusted courtiers. But he too had been divorced. Princess Margaret too was faced with a stark choice. She chose her duty, and she and the Group Captain had to part.

When you contrast those two pieces of history with the present day, you realise how our attitudes to divorce have changed over a few short decades. Princess Margaret herself was divorced from her husband in 1978. Three out of the Queen's four children have been married and all three have been through the heartbreak and trauma of marital breakdown. Sadly none of this is very unusual as one in every three marriages now ends in divorce.

But, perhaps rather surprisingly, the high rate of marriage breakdown does not seem to be discouraging people. Now more than a third of all marriages celebrated are marriages where the husband, the wife, or both partners are having another shot at marital bliss. And some of those husbands and wives are trying for the third, fourth or even fifth time!

It is difficult to say why so many marriages are breaking down today. When most people were committed to a religion and attended a church regularly their marriages were bolstered by their faith. Marriage was a sacrament, an undertaking until death parted.

Only the church had any power over marriage in those days. Divorce was a possibility but quite rare. In the time of Henry VIII a divorce could be obtained, as Henry's well-known exploits demonstrate, but a divorce was certainly not an option for anyone but the extremely rich and influential. Henry wanted to divorce his first queen so that he could marry the fascinating Anne Boleyn, partly because he had fallen in love with Anne but also partly because he had no son and heir and hoped that Anne would be able to produce one for him.

The problem for Henry was that only the Pope in Rome could grant a divorce. The Pope, for reasons not unconnected with European politics, was not prepared to help Henry with his plan. Henry, in a temper, declared himself head of the church in England and granted himself his own divorce. Even for hundreds of years after that, a divorce could only be had through the church courts at enormous expense and as a result of a very slow process.

No doubt some marriages were unhappy. But most people had very little expectation of married happiness in those days. Marriages were usually arranged between the families of the bride and groom. The young people themselves would have had very little say in the arrangements. Remarriage was fairly common, and that was because people generally had a much shorter life span. Childbirth was a risky business and many mothers simply did not survive it. Medicine was in its infancy and most diseases were just incurable. As a result, a husband or wife lucky enough to enjoy good health might outlive several spouses and remarry several times.

Most of us live much longer today. It is not all that unusual for happily married couples to live to celebrate their golden and even their diamond wedding anniversaries. For those lucky enough to have found happiness, these are real occasions for celebrating. But for unhappily married people, the prospect of sixty years of togetherness can sound more like a life sentence.

Even when divorce had become something which the civil courts decided rather than a matter for the church, a husband and a wife did not come to the court on anything like equal terms. First, the husband was usually the one with the money, so that he would have been the one who was able to afford to try for a divorce. But even when a wife could afford to try to get a divorce she was treated differently. A husband could get a divorce simply on the ground that his wife had committed adultery. But if a wife wanted a divorce because of her husband's adultery she had to prove that the adultery had been incestuous, or had been coupled with bigamy, rape, sodomy, bestiality or cruelty.

If a woman who had children was found to have committed adultery, she could say goodbye to the children for ever, no matter how young they were. But a father who had committed adultery would not have had to suffer separation from his children. Children belonged to their fathers, who could do pretty much as they pleased with them.

If you were asking for a divorce and you had committed adultery yourself you might be refused the divorce. If you were a divorced person you were someone to be avoided, especially if you happened to be a woman. The person who had been divorced was particularly shunned as being the "guilty" party.

Irretrievable Breakdown

In 1969 an attempt was made to get rid of the idea that there had to be a guilty party in every divorce case. It was decided that the only ground for a divorce should be the irretrievable breakdown of the marriage – in other words that there could only be a divorce in cases where there was no hope whatsoever of the marriage surviving. But unfortunately Parliament then went on to decide that the breakdown had to be shown in one of five ways. The ways in which breakdown could be shown were to be adultery, unreasonable behaviour, desertion for two years, living apart for two years if both partners agreed to a divorce, and living apart for five years, even if one of the partners did not want a divorce.

To be accused of committing adultery or of behaving so unreasonably that someone should not be expected to live with you have, not surprisingly, continued to inflame emotions. Going through a divorce is still one of the most stressful experiences which anyone can have, and being branded as the guilty party just makes matters worse. The truth is that in far and away the majority of divorces there is no guilty party and no innocent party. Marriages break down for all sorts of reasons, but it usually takes two to break a marriage just as it takes two to make one successful.

If we could get rid of the notions of guilt and innocence in marriage breakdown it could help lessen the grief and bitterness which most divorcing couples experience. Even more importantly, it could relieve some of the desperate unhappiness experienced by the countless numbers of children unlucky enough to be caught up in the crossfire between warring parents. The Lord Chancellor has brought out some suggestions of ways in which divorce laws could be improved to eliminate the ideas of guilt and innocence. Details of his suggestions are set out in Chapter 3.

Divorce and Legal Separation Today

Today one in every three marriages in this country ends in breakdown. If you are involved in a divorce yourself or if you have been, you will know that behind this bland statistic is hidden an unimaginable amount of human misery. People who go through marriage breakdown feel disappointment, anger, bitterness, grief, rejection and inadequacy. On top of all that, there is the sense of utter loneliness and isolation. After all, you have invested your whole self in this relationship. Whatever it is that has gone wrong, your self confidence must have taken quite a knock. The grief is very similar to that of bereavement by death. This is not surprising, for the death of a relationship is often just as shattering as the loss of a close friend or family member.

Unfortunately, when there are children of the marriage, they are likely to suffer even more than their parents. Adults can try to make sense of what has happened, to find explanations. Children only know that their world has suddenly come to an end, when the two people who mean security and love to them decide that they no longer love one another. There is no way that a young child can possibly grasp the issues involved in marital breakdown. All he or she knows is that happiness has been destroyed. Child psychiatrists have discovered that children often blame themselves when their parents split up. To an adult that may seem laughable, but the effect on a child can be lifelong.

Why Do So Many Marriages Break Up Today?

No one really knows why so many marriages break up. Some experts think that young people are simply not being given enough proper preparation for adult relationships, including marriage. It may be that we should be concentrating more on training for adult relationships in schools, where the mechanics of sex education are often taught in complete isolation from other aspects of relating to other people which are just as important.

No relationship between two people is ever going to be completely without problems. But "it's the bad times that make the good times", as the Irish expression has it. Every couple lucky enough to have enjoyed a lasting relationship can look back over their years together and identify bad times, when the going got really rough, and one or both partners might have felt like giving it all up. But the fact that they did get through those times together will mean that their relationship has grown in strength as a result.

When things go wrong, divorce sometimes seems to be the easy solution. It may well be that our law has gone too far in making it such an easy option. When the divorce laws were reformed in the 1960s nobody really expected that the divorce rate would rise as spectacularly as it has. It was thought that there might be an increase in divorce figures immediately, because many couples had been trapped for years in loveless unions from which there was no escape. But after an initial rise in divorce figures, it was forecast that the divorce rate would settle down. Sadly, the annual numbers of divorces have been increasing ever since.

A solicitor acting for someone who was filing a petition for divorce had to give a certificate which said whether or not the possibility of a reconciliation had been discussed with the client before the petition was filed. The idea was to ensure that reconciliation had always been raised as a possibility before the divorce was applied for. It was hoped that this might prevent a couple rushing into a divorce without thinking matters through properly.

But solicitors would almost always file certificates which stated that the possibility of a reconciliation had *not* been discussed with the client. Solicitors are busy people. They do not generally see themselves as counsellors or marriage guidance experts. They might think that by the time someone had arrived at their offices to ask about getting a divorce it was probably far too late to start talking about reconciliation. That may sometimes be right. But it is a great pity that so many divorces go through without any attempt being made to see whether there is some other way to get round the problems in the marriage. This is obviously particularly true when there are any children, whose lives are going to be so shattered if there is to be a divorce.

Help with Problems

Anyone thinking about a divorce should first consider whether there is any possibility that expert counselling might be able to help. No matter how black things may look to you, it may well be that there is a way to save your relationship. You meant enough to one another to make the enormous commitment of getting married, maybe the even more important commitment of having children together. It is at least possible that you might be able to find that closeness again.

The first thing to realise is that the marriage in which there have never been problems is something which does not exist. It is not an admission of failure if you are having difficulties. But if things are going wrong you are likely to feel confused and unhappy, uncertain about what will be the right thing to do.

Help is at hand. Relate, which used to be called the Marriage Guidance Council, provides the principal counselling service for people having problems with relationships. Relate has about 400 centres throughout the country and over fifty years of experience in helping couples in trouble. Relate offers counselling to couples whether they are married or unmarried.

People are often worried by the idea of asking for counselling about their marriage. They wonder what the counsellors will be like. They may be put off by the idea that an interview with a counsellor will be like being summoned to the headmaster's study at school. They wonder if they will be treated as though they were neurotic or highly strung or stupid.

Relate counsellors are carefully selected and then trained for two years. Their training teaches them what makes relationships work – and what works against good relationships. They do not adopt a superior attitude. They do not "tell people off", act as judges or preach. Unshockable, they are trained above all to listen.

The atmosphere at Relate centres is as relaxed and friendly as possible, with paper hankies at the ready. The problems people bring to the counsellors are as varied as the people themselves – inability to talk to a partner or to persuade a partner to talk to them perhaps, loneliness, jealousy, problems with children or in-laws. All these are just some examples of common difficulties.

Relate emphasise that the time to come for counselling, if possible, is when problems first arise. Waiting for them to resolve themselves may mean that by the time counselling is sought it is really too late because things have got themselves into such a terrible mess. But that does not mean that counselling can never help when problems have existed for a long time. People can be helped at any stage.

The address and telephone number of the national headquarters of Relate are listed at the end of the chapter. Your local telephone directory should have the number of your local Relate centre where you can make an appointment for an initial interview. At that interview the counsellor will discuss the best kind of help for you. It might be that only two or three sessions will be necessary to help. You might need more.

Obviously, if both you and your partner go together counselling is likely to be more successful. But even if your partner refuses to go, counselling can often help. If things do begin to improve between you as a result of the counselling sessions, your partner might be persuaded to come with you. Although you are asked to make a contribution if you can afford it, counselling is free to anyone unable to pay.

What the counsellor does during the sessions is to try to help you to understand your relationship, the problems which have come up and the possible causes for them, and the various choices available to you as solutions. The counsellor then helps you to work out your own answers to the problems. He or she does not tell you what to do. It is for you to consider the options open to you and to choose the one which seems best.

Mediation

Counsellors will not try to persuade you to stay together. They know how damaging a divorce can be, especially when there are children in the family, but they are realistic. They recognise that there is no hope for some relationships. If a marriage must end, the counsellor is trained to help the couple to separate with less anger and bitterness and to reach a fair and friendly settlement of matters concerning their children and any property which they own.

If you decide to go ahead with a divorce you will obviously hope to minimise feelings of anger and bitterness in any areas where there might be disputes between you, over with whom the children should live, or what should happen to your home, for example. Counsellors are trained in mediation skills and can help separating partners to decide together what will be the best solution to problems about their children or money or property matters. As they are completely independent, no one need feel that a counsellor is "on the other person's side".

In addition to Relate, counselling is provided by such organisations as the Catholic Marriage Advisory Council, the Jewish Marriage Council, and One Plus One; you will find a list of addresses and telephone numbers at the end of this chapter.

Lawyers may not always seem the most helpful people when two people are splitting up; they do have a reputation for raising the temperature in divorce cases. However, this reputation is not entirely deserved. There are some lawyers who most certainly do write letters and conduct cases in a way which can only aggravate already explosive situations. But the majority of lawyers who specialise in family law are dedicated to keeping acrimony out of family disputes as far as they possibly can.

All committed family lawyers try to help people to reach sensible agreements rather than having court battles, if at all possible. The Family Mediators Association trains solicitors, barristers and other suitably qualified professionals in mediation techniques to enable them to help partners to come to agreements in areas of dispute.

Mediation is not an attempt to persuade parties to have a reconciliation. It accepts that there will be a divorce and simply concentrates on helping people to reach sensible agreements.

How to Get a Divorce

If you have been forced to the conclusion that there is no hope for your marriage and you want to be divorced it is not all that difficult to do it all yourself. But if there are going to be arguments about children or property it will probably be necessary to go to a solicitor.

A series of helpful leaflets about divorce have been published by the Lord Chancellor's Department. Copies of the leaflets can be obtained at your local county court or Citizens Advice Bureau (addresses in the telephone book).

Firstly, you must fill in a form called a "petition". These forms are free and can be obtained from your local county court. The court staff should be friendly and helpful, but they are not lawyers and cannot give legal advice on any questions you might have about the petition. You can start the divorce process in any divorce county court or in the Principal Registry of the Family Division of the High Court.

You cannot petition for a divorce unless you have been married for more than one year. Once you have issued a petition you will be called "the petitioner" by the court and your husband or wife will be called "the respondent".

You, or your husband or wife, must be living permanently in England or Wales on the date when the petition is started, or one of you must have been living in England or Wales for at least a year on the day the petition is filed (ie. left at the counter).

At the moment the fee for starting a petition is £40 although it does change from time to time. Court staff will be able to tell you the current amount. Once you have obtained a divorce, you may also have to pay a further fee of £15 for a copy of the divorce decree.

If everything is straightforward you will not need to go to a solicitor. But you may have to consult a solicitor if you are not sure whether you have grounds for a divorce. These will be explained below.

You might have to go to a solicitor if, for example, your husband or wife is not likely to agree to the divorce, or if you have not been able to agree about who the children should live with or how often they should see the parent with whom they are not living. Again, if there are going to be arguments about property or money, you may have to go for some legal advice.

If you are being advised by a solicitor under the legal aid "Green Form" scheme (for further information on this see Chapter 16) or if you are receiving income support or family credit you will not have to pay the £40 to issue the petition or the £15 to get a copy of the decree.

Legal aid

If you are eligible for legal aid it does not automatically mean that all your legal fees will be met by the legal aid fund. If, for example, you decide to ask the court to make an order for financial support or about the matrimonial home or about some question relating to your children, you may find at the end of the day that you will have to pay back all the cost of the legal proceedings to the legal aid fund. This is only likely to happen if you get a lump sum or an interest in property as a result of the proceedings. For more information about legal costs see Chapter 16.

Grounds for divorce

The only way to get a divorce in this country is to prove to the satisfaction of the court that your marriage has broken down irretrievably, in other words that there is no hope for it. There are five possible ways to prove that a marriage has irretrievably broken down.

Adultery

You must prove that your husband or wife has committed adultery. If you know the name of the person with whom the adultery has been committed you must put the name in your petition. That person will then become the "co-respondent".

If you are relying on your husband's or wife's adultery in your petition the court must also be satisfied that you "find it intolerable to live with" him or her, meaning you can no longer stand the situation of living together.

The odd thing is that you can, in fact, live with your husband or wife for up to six months after the adultery and still be granted a decree. But if you live together for more than six months after the adultery you cannot petition for a divorce on the basis of the adultery.

"Living together" means as husband and wife. Obviously, there are situations where people simply have to go on living under the same roof even after the marriage has completely broken down. If they are living separate lives under the same roof that does not count as "living together".

But usually it will be enough for a decree to be granted if your husband or wife admits the adultery.

Unreasonable behaviour

This is the most "popular" ground in petitions. You have to prove that your husband or wife has behaved so badly that it is not reasonable that you should be expected to live with him or her.

An obvious example of such behaviour would be where a husband or wife has been physically violent to the other person and has caused injury. But the behaviour need not be as bad as that, although it needs to be reasonably serious.

Even so, behaviour which seems unbearable to one person may be quite acceptable to someone else. One man got a divorce because his wife gave the cats better meals than she gave him. A woman succeeded in persuading a court that her husband was unreasonable because his do-it-yourself efforts around the house were conducted at a snail's pace, leaving her to cope over many months with such inconveniences as a doorless toilet.

Desertion

You would be entitled to a divorce if your husband or wife had walked out on you at least two years ago and had not returned.

Living apart for two years with consent

If you and your husband or wife have been living apart for at least two years and you *both agree* that you want to divorce you will be entitled to.

Again, "living apart" can include living separately under the same roof. If you have been sleeping in separate rooms, eating your meals separately, not doing things like washing or cooking for one another and not going out socially together that can count as living apart even though you have been living at the same address.

Living apart for five years

Where a husband and wife have been living apart for at least five years, either of them can apply for a divorce whether or not the other agrees.

What you will need to do

You will need to collect three copies of form D8 (divorce petition) from a divorce county court office or from the Principal Registry of the Family Division in London. Offices are open from 10 a.m. until 4 p.m. Monday to Friday, apart from bank holidays. Telephone books have the addresses of county courts or you can enquire at a Citizens Advice Bureau or a post office for the address.

One copy of form D8 is for you to keep, one copy is for the court and one copy is for the court to send to your husband or wife. If your petition is on the ground of adultery and you know the name of the other person (the co-respondent) you will need an extra copy of form D8 for the court to serve on the co-respondent.

The court will give you some notes to help you fill in the petition. You can also get a form D92 to fill in if you do not have to pay fees because you are on income support or receive family credit.

Information you need

Aside from your own name and address you must have the full name and address of your husband or wife and the full names and dates of birth of any living children you have, no matter how old they are.

If you are relying on adultery you will need the full name and address of the person with whom the adultery was committed. If you do not have this information, you can still name the person. For example if your husband had told you that he had committed adultery with someone called Mary, you can put "known to the petitioner only as Mary".

You must send your marriage certificate (not a photocopy) with the petition. If you have lost your marriage certificate you can apply for another one at St Catherine's House, Kingsway, London WC2.

If you feel that you still need help with the forms, you can take them to a Citizens Advice Bureau. However, people who will help you there are not trained lawyers and will not be able to give you legal advice. If you need the help of a solicitor you may be able to get it under what is called the "Green Form" scheme. Not every firm of solicitors will give this type of advice. Those who are prepared to advise legally aided clients will have the "Legal Aid" logo displayed somewhere so that you can recognise them.

After the petition has been filed

The court will send a copy of the petition to your husband or wife, and to the co-respondent (the person with whom adultery has been committed) if there is one. The respondent (your husband or wife) and the co-respondent, if any, will be given eight days to let the court know that the petition has been received.

The document which is sent to the court by respondents is called an "acknowledgment of service" (form D10). The court will send you a copy of this.

If the address you gave the court is incorrect, possibly because the respondent or co-respondent has moved, the Post Office will return the forms to the court. The court will inform you about this. If you want to carry on with the divorce you will have to find out the correct address and let the court have it. The court will then post the forms to the new address.

What the respondent can do

When your petition is sent by the court, your husband or wife (the respondent) and the co-respondent (if there is one) may react in one of three ways.

Some people simply ignore the petition, or tear it up and put it in the rubbish bin. Others fill in their form D10 and tell the court that they do not agree with your petition and intend to fight it.

The third possibility is what happens most often. Most husbands and wives are not taken by surprise when they receive a petition as they will probably have already discussed the divorce with their partners. Others may just be ready to agree that the marriage has broken down irretrievably. Those people simply fill in the form D10 saying that they agree with the petition and then return the form to the court.

If form D10 is returned to the court in your case the court will send you a copy. The Lord Chancellor's Leaflet 4, which can be obtained at the divorce county court, tells you what to do next.

What happens if the respondent does not return D10?

When eight days have passed since the petition was sent and no form D10 has come back, the court will send you two copies of another form. This requests the court to send its representative, called "the bailiff", to give a copy of the petition to the respondent personally.

You will have to fill in the forms and return them to the court. With them you must send a photograph of the respondent, if possible. If not, you must give a written description of him or her, mentioning the approximate height, the colour of eyes and hair, and what sort of build the person is physically. Any other characteristic which might help a stranger to recognise him or her should be mentioned, for example "walks with a limp".

You will have to pay a fee of £5 for each person to be served, unless you are on income support or receiving family credit.

It will not matter if a co-respondent cannot be found or will not co-operate as long as the court is satisfied that reasonable efforts have been made to inform him or her of the allegation.

What happens next

When the court sends copies of the acknowledgment (form D10) you must check what the respondent or co-respondent has written in answer to the question "Do you intend to defend the case?"

If the answer to that question is "no" you can then ask the court to consider whether you have grounds for a divorce and whether the arrangements that you are suggesting for your children are satisfactory. This is called "applying for directions for trial".

If the respondent or co-respondent answers "yes" you must wait for twenty-nine days from the day they say they received your petition. This is the period during which they must file their defence to the petition which is called an "answer".

If after twenty-nine days you have not received a copy of an answer, you can then apply for directions for trial.

If you do receive an answer to your petition you should ask the advice of a solicitor about how to deal with it.

The final procedure

You will need copies of forms D84 and D80 which can be obtained free of charge from the court office. There are different kinds of form D80 depending upon which ground you have relied upon in your petition. Make sure you are given the form which matches up to your ground – adultery, behaviour and so on.

When you have filled in both forms you can send or take them to the court office, but not before nine days have passed since the respondent (and any co-respondent) say they received your petition.

Form D80 is an affidavit, which means that you have to swear that what you have written in it is true in front of someone who is qualified to witness you signing the affidavit. This means that you must not sign D80 until you are in the presence of a solicitor or an officer of the court or Principal Registry.

A solicitor will charge £3.50 plus £1 for every document attached ("exhibited") to your affidavit. A list of the documents which should be attached and full explanations about filling in the forms are given in the Lord Chancellor's Leaflet 4.

Getting the divorce

All the papers connected with your case will be given to a judge. The judge considers all the papers and decides if you can have a divorce. You do not need to come to court when this is done.

If you have children the judge will carefully consider the arrangements which you are proposing to make for them and which you have set out in the documents.

If the judge decides to grant you a divorce the court will send you, your husband or wife, and any co-respondent a certificate saying that you are entitled to a decree. On the certificate will be a time and date for the "pronouncement" of the decree. There is no need to attend court for this. The name of the case is read out, usually with a list of other cases, and the judge simply says that he pronounces a decree.

You will then be sent a document called a "decree nisi". Although this is a divorce decree it does not mean that you are finally divorced. You are not finally divorced until the decree has been made "absolute".

You can normally obtain your decree absolute six weeks after the date of the decree nisi. Sometimes, where there are children of the family, the court will hold up the decree absolute for longer than six weeks so that matters concerning the children can be considered. If the court is going to do this you will be informed.

You need yet another form to make your decree absolute and again you can obtain it from the court office. The fee when you apply for decree absolute is £15 at the moment, although it changes from time to time. Court staff will tell you what it is. If you are on income support or in receipt of famiy credit you will not have to pay anything.

Judicial separation

It may be that for some reason, religious beliefs for example, you would prefer a judicial separation to a divorce. Judicial separations can be obtained on the same grounds as those for divorce.

Religious marriages

Roman Catholics, Jews, Muslims and members of other religions may wish to apply for a religious dissolution of their marriage in addition to a civil divorce. Some useful addresses are given at the end of the chapter.

Defended divorces

Most divorces are now undefended, which means that the respondent allows the petition to go ahead. This does not mean, of course, that most respondents agree with what is said in the divorce petition. On the contrary, the majority of respondents deeply resent the allegations made against them in the petition and sincerely believe that they are at best wild exaggerations.

The sole ground for divorce in this country is that the marriage has irretrievably broken down. In some countries it is sufficient to establish that both parties agree that the marriage has broken down for a divorce to be granted.

In this country, it is not sufficient for the parties simply to agree that their marriage has broken down irretrievably for a divorce to be granted, unless they have been living apart for two years.

Somewhat unfortunately, our divorce law contains a requirement that the irretrievable breakdown of a marriage should be proved in one of five specific ways. These are adultery, unreasonable behaviour, desertion for a period of two years, living apart for two years if both parties agree, and living apart for five years.

Perhaps not too surprisingly, it is the unreasonable behaviour petitions which really cause the problems. The formal wording of the petition claims that the respondent has behaved in such a way that it is unreasonable for the petitioner to be expected to live with him or her. It is understandably hurtful to be told that you have behaved so badly that your wife or husband should not be expected to live with you any more.

The natural reaction is to want to retaliate. "I may have done that, but what about the time she . . .?" Or, "Put in those words what I did looks pretty terrible, but let's face it, there was quite a bit of provocation."

The first reaction for many respondents, when they receive a petition making allegations about their behaviour, is that they want to defend, or even to cross petition for divorce themselves. But when they ask about this, they will almost invariably be advised that they should allow the petition to proceed undefended. This is very good advice.

Defending a petition can be an extremely costly business. You might, of course, think of defending it in person, without instructing a lawyer. It is possible. A few people actually do it. But what you must bear in mind is that if you are not successful in defending the petition, even if you avoid paying lawyers to represent you, the court can still make an order for costs against you. This would mean that you would have to pay all the costs of the petitioner, including the cost of lawyers.

A very common anxiety for respondents to petitions based on behaviour is that the allegations made against them, if allowed to go undefended, might count against them when it comes to a dispute about the future of the children of the family, or about finance. However, it is possible to make it clear, when acknowledging service of a petition and indicating no intention to defend, that this is on a "without prejudice" basis and that you reserve the right to dispute the allegations when other matters are being considered by the court.

Another possibility, if there is one particularly wounding allegation, something about behaviour towards a child of the family for example, is to try to get the petitioner to agree to delete that allegation, on the basis that you will allow the petition to proceed undefended if that allegation is taken out.

It is, of course, always important to remember that even when a petition has been filed it is still not too late for the marriage to be saved. Skilled counselling can still be tried, if both parties to the marriage are willing to attempt a reconciliation. Sometimes it is only when a respondent actually reads the petition, and sees what is upsetting the petitioner to the point of wanting a divorce, that he or she realises how serious the problems have become. It might not be too late. It is nearly always worth considering whether you really want to part, especially if you have children.

All that having been said, there are still some respondents who do not feel able to allow the petition to go undefended. They want to defend, either on the basis that they have not committed the adultery alleged or that they have not done the other things which the petition alleges amount to unreasonable behaviour.

A respondent can choose simply to defend, to say that the marriage has not broken down irretrievably because the allegations made in the petition are untrue. On the other hand, a respondent can agree that the marriage has broken down irretrievably but deny that he or she is at fault and say that the breakdown is all the fault of the petitioner. The respondent then makes allegations against the petitioner, of adultery or of unreasonable behaviour. This is called cross petitioning.

Whether the respondent is simply defending or is defending and cross petitioning the matter has to go to court and be heard by a judge.

Useful Addresses

National Association of Family Mediation and Conciliation Services,
50 Westminster Bridge Road,
London SE1 7QY
Tel: 071 721 7658

Family Mediators Association (FMA),
The Old House,
Rectory Gardens,
Henbury,
Bristol BS10 7AQ
Tel: 0272 500140

Divorce Conciliation and Advisory Service (DCAS),
38 Ebury Street, London SW1 0LU
Tel: 071 730 2422

Relate,
Herbert Gray College,
Little Church Street,
Rugby, Warwickshire CV21 3AP
Tel: 0788 573241

Catholic Marriage Advisory Council (CMAC),
Clitherow House,
1 Blythe Mews, Blythe Road
London W14 0NW
Tel: 071 371 1341

Jewish Marriage Council,
23 Ravenshurst Avenue,
London NW4 4EE
Tel: 081 203 6311 Crisis Helpline: 0345 581999

Asian Family Counselling Service,
74 The Avenue,
London W13 8LB.
Tel: 081 997 5749; and
6A South Road, Southall UB1 1RT
Tel: 081 813 8321

The Family Welfare Association,
501–505 Kingsland Road,
London E8 4AU
Tel: 071 254 6251

National Council for the Divorced and Separated,
13 High Street,
Little Shelford,
Cambridge CB2 5ES
Tel: 0533 708880

One Plus One,
Central Middlesex Hospital,
Acton Lane,
London NW10 7NS
Tel: 081 965 236

Solicitors Family Law Association (SFLA),
PO Box 302,
Keston,
Kent BR2 6EZ
Tel: 0689 85022

Your local Citizens Advice Bureau (address and number in telephone directory) can also help; or try
National Association of Citizens Advice Bureaux (NACAB),
115–123 Pentonville Road,
London N1 9LZ
Tel: 071 833 2181

Principal Registry of the Family Division
Somerset House,
Strand,
London
WC2R 1LP

National Council for the Divorced and Separated
13 High Street,
Little Shelford,
Cambridge
CB2 5ES

British Association of Counselling,
37A Sheep Street,
Rugby,
Warwickshire
CV21 3BX
Tel: 0788 78328/9

If you are already divorced, separated or widowed, support and advice is available from:

The Beginning Experience,
1 Apple Tree Walk,
Clymping,
Near Littlehampton
West Sussex BN17 5QN
Tel: 0903 722230

2

WHO GETS WHAT WHEN YOU SPLIT UP?

Questions about money and property tend to come up in almost every relationship breakdown. In some cases, of course, there is no difficulty. If two people have been married or living together in rented accommodation, they have no children and each of them has a job, there should be no difficulties about finances or property when their relationship founders. But in most relationships the financial facts are not quite so straightforward. For example, when only one partner has been in employment, with the other staying at home to care for their children throughout the relationship, or when they have been purchasing a house or flat on a mortgage, someone has to decide who gets what when they separate. It is a hard but inescapable fact of life that two households are not going to be able to live as cheaply as one did.

If your relationship is breaking down and you have decided to separate, the first step is to see whether you can agree between you what is to happen about finance and about any property which you may own. If you can't agree, you should definitely attempt to get some mediator or conciliator to help you. Why? One good reason is that to reach agreement with the help of mediation will be much cheaper than asking the court to decide what should happen. Even if you are legally aided, you still have to meet the costs of lawyers and a court hearing yourself in the end, if you are awarded more than £2,500 at the end of the proceedings. But if you can't even reach agreement with the help of mediation, the law is the last resort.

Married Couples

It used to be the case that if a married woman owned any property or earned any money, it belonged to her husband. It is less than a hundred and fifty years since the law began to give a wife some rights over her own finances. The courts can now make orders that one partner in a marriage – usually the husband but it can be the wife – should make regular payments for the maintenance of the other. The courts can also make orders for dividing between the husband and wife any capital assets, such as houses, flats or savings.

Even if you have not actually filed a divorce petition, you can still obtain an order for maintenance in a court if your husband (or wife) should support you and is refusing.

Since the Child Support law came into force in 1993, things have changed completely so far as the maintenance of children is concerned. Deciding how much maintenance should be paid for a child and making a parent pay that amount is now under the control of a government agency, the Child Support Agency. The courts no longer come into the picture so far as maintenance of children is concerned, unless there are very exceptional circumstances. Child Support is discussed fully in Chapter 9.

What are your rights to money and property if your marriage ends?

When a marriage has broken down the law has given the court power to make any orders about finances or property which seem to the court to be just. The power of the court includes the power to order that maintenance payments should be made by one ex-partner to the other. The court can also make orders which affect property or other capital assets which one or both of the partners to the marriage may own. In most cases, of course, the most important asset which a couple have is the home in which they have lived together.

That home may be in the sole name of the husband. He alone may have provided the deposit when it was purchased, and he may have paid off the instalments on the mortgage entirely from his own earnings. He might have other capital assets, savings in a building society for example, a boat or an expensive car. He might own his own business and have a great deal of capital invested in that.

Less often, the wife may be wealthy in her own right. She may own property, or valuable jewellery, for example. She could be a successful businesswoman or a professional woman with capital assets or substantial savings.

The court will look at every bit of property or capital owned by the husband and by the wife. It then looks at the facts of the particular marriage to help it decide what orders it can make which will be fair to everyone. When it does so, it has to keep in mind that, if there are any children of the marriage, the interests of the children will be the most important consideration. This means, for example, that the parent who has the children living with him or her will be more likely to keep the home, at least until the children have all reached the age of seventeen.

What does the court take into account?

When a court has to make decisions about money or property (ancillary matters, as they are called) there are certain things which have to be taken into account by law. If a judge should make an order about money or property which does not properly consider all these matters the order would be appealable.

1 Resources

The first thing which a judge must do when he is deciding how money or property ought to be divided after a divorce is to look at the resources of the husband and the wife. The resources will include the income of each, the earning capacity which each has and any property which each of them owns. It is important to remember that, when the court is considering earning capacity, it does not simply look at what each partner is earning at the time when the matter comes before the court. Often, the wife will not have been earning money for some years because she has been looking after young children. If the children have all started at school, for example, the judge might decide that the mother has skills which give her an earning capacity, even if it is only to be on a part-time basis. If the mother happened to have some qualification, in teaching or nursing perhaps, that would be taken into account. Or it might be possible for the mother to undergo some training to improve skills which she already has, such as secretarial skills, in order to get her into the job market again.

However, the court will always look at all the facts. A mother who has not been in employment for twenty years will not be expected to go straight out and earn her own living. The ages of her children will be an important consideration and the state of the job market in her locality will also be taken into account.

The court will also consider resources which either the husband or the wife are likely to have in the foreseeable future. Two such examples are illustrated in the following case studies.

CASE STUDY

Marjorie and Kenneth are divorcing, having been married for nine years. They have two young children, who will be living with Marjorie. They have always lived in rented accommodation and neither of them has any substantial capital or savings. Kenneth's wealthy aunt died shortly after he and Marjorie separated. Under the terms of his aunt's will Kenneth has been left £100,000, which he will receive in the near future. Can Marjorie expect to be awarded some of that money by the court?

The answer is that in all those circumstances it is likely that Marjorie would be given a lump sum by the court to be paid by Kenneth from his expected inheritance. That £100,000 is a resource which he is likely, indeed certain, to have in the foreseeable future and it can consequently be brought into consideration by the court.

On the other hand, had Kenneth's wealthy aunt been a woman still in her fifties and in excellent health, it is unlikely that the court would take Kenneth's prospects of an inheritance from her into account. She might not leave him anything at all in her will and she might well live for another thirty years or more.

CASE STUDY

Julie and Tim are divorcing after nine years of marriage. They have no children. Tim has always been the breadwinner while Julie stayed at home as a housewife throughout the marriage. Julie is asking the court to order that Tim should pay maintenance for her. Since their separation, a few months ago, Julie has been doing a course in bookkeeping. She is doing well on the course and expects to qualify as a bookkeeper in six months' time. The court will take into account the fact that Julie can reasonably be expected to get her bookkeeping qualifications and then to find a job so that she can support herself. If the court is satisfied that bookkeeping jobs will be available within a reasonable distance of where Julie is living, the order for Tim to pay her maintenance may well take account of the situation by providing for the payments to be made only for a certain length of time, say twelve months, to give Julie a chance to get on her feet and be self-supporting.

Every case is unique, of course, and there are many other important considerations for the court, so that Marjorie, Kenneth, Julie and Tim can only be examples of what might happen.

2 Needs, obligations and responsibilities

Once the court has determined the resources of a husband and wife, the needs, obligations and responsibilities of each has to be taken into account. The most obvious need for anyone is some sort of roof over his or her head. The court will do its utmost to try to ensure that both husband and wife have a home at the end of the day.

Desirable as it is for each of the divorcing partners to have a home, this cannot always be achieved. If there are children of the family, the court will always give priority to providing a home for them. This means that the parent with whom the children are to live will almost always be the one who will be allowed to remain in the former matrimonial home where there is not enough money to provide two homes.

Because the mother is often, although not by any means always, the parent with whom the children will live, it is often the mother who stays in the matrimonial home. This has given rise to a view, fairly common among fathers, that the courts favour mothers when it comes to financial matters in divorce proceedings.

The courts try to be as fair as possible, while remaining mindful that the needs of the children have to come first. In many cases the mother will be allowed to stay in the home with the children, but only until the children are of school leaving age. At that stage, the court may say that the home should be sold and the net proceeds divided between the husband and wife in whatever proportions the court considers just.

It cannot be said too often that every case has its own individual set of facts. This means that it is impossible to be certain about what might or might not happen in any particular case. There are so many factors to be taken into account that the best that can be attempted is an "educated guess".

3 Contributions

The court will take into account the contributions to the marriage made by the husband and the wife. The husband may have made all the financial contributions and might think that, because of that, the wife should not be entitled to claim anything.

But in many marriages where the husband has been the sole earner and contributor of money the wife has played her part by bringing up the children, cleaning, washing, ironing and cooking for all the family, and generally carrying out all the work lumped together as "being a housewife".

The courts take the view that the sort of contribution made by a wife who stays at home to care for the home, the husband and their children is equally as important as that of the man who goes out and earns the money.

4 Age

The ages of the husband and wife can affect the decision of the court about financial matters.

CASE STUDY

Doreen, a fifty-five-year-old wife, has stayed at home caring for her family for thirty years. In that time her husband Frank, who is the same age, has built up his own reasonably profitable business, from the proceeds of which he has supported Doreen and their family. It will be difficult, if not impossible, for Frank to persuade the court that Doreen ought to go out and get a job and be self-supporting to relieve him of the liability to maintain her in the future.

It has been said by the courts that "marriage is not a meal ticket for life". Although this reflects the court's hope that partners to a broken marriage can eventually become financially independent of one another, judges are realists. Women of fifty-five, with no special qualifications or skills and out of the job market for thirty years, are not likely to be able to find jobs in today's conditions.

Doreen has made her contribution to the marriage over the years. Unless Frank is in a financial position to pay her a large sum of money to compensate her for loss of maintenance in the future, his liability to maintain her would be likely to continue.

The length of the marriage is important too.

CASE STUDY

Ben is a millionaire. He meets Audrey, who has no money at all. They marry, but very quickly realise that the marriage is a mistake and separate after only a year. There are no children. Can Audrey expect substantial financial provision from Ben?

The answer will almost certainly be no although she might get an order for a limited period if she needs time to find a job.

5 Is behaviour taken into account?

People are in a very vulnerable state at the time of the breakdown of their relationship. Often, extremely hurtful things are said and done, because when you are hurt yourself you usually feel like giving as good as you get. The husband, the wife, or even both, may behave in quite outrageous ways. When money and property cases come before the court, it is sometimes difficult for people to resist the temptation to tell the court all about the rotten behaviour of the other person. Husbands or wives often seem to believe that if their partner has behaved badly that ought to affect the amount of money to be awarded by the court.

But the court is only allowed to take conduct into account in a very limited way. The behaviour must be so bad that a reasonable person would say that it would be unjust for the court to ignore it. This standard is a high one, and it means that only in a very few cases will the behaviour of one of the partners be taken into account when it comes to deciding on a division of money or property.

In one case the wife had actually assisted the husband's attempts at suicide, because she was hoping that she would benefit financially on his death. At the same time she had been committing adultery. That behaviour was found by the court to satisfy the test. The wife's entitlement to financial provision was reduced because of it.

But in another case, where a wife had been committing adultery with a boy half her age, who was a guest in the matrimonial home, the judge decided that the wife's behaviour was not bad enough for him to take it into account when deciding financial matters.

6 All the circumstances

The matters listed above are just some of the important things which the court must take into account when deciding financial and property cases in divorce but they are by no means the only things which will be considered. The law requires that the judge take into account *all* the circumstances in any particular case, and as every case is unique it means that advising on financial matters in divorce is not at all an easy task.

Also remember that judges are human beings, with their own, very often unconscious, prejudices and opinions. The vast majority of them are skilled professionals and are dedicated to being as fair as they can be to both parties in any case which comes before them. That does not mean, however, that there is only one obvious outcome to every case.

Reaching an agreement without going to court

It is quite impossible for anyone to be absolutely certain of what the court will decide in any particular case. It is therefore extremely important for you to think very carefully about whether you can possibly come to an agreement about your money and property when you divorce. This avoids the uncertainty, the delay – and the considerable expense! – of a court hearing.

Agreements have another advantage. It is unlikely that either the husband or the wife will get exactly what he or she has been hoping for, as a result of the agreement. But at least, even if each has been a little disappointed, at the same time a compromise has been reached which each is prepared to accept.

Once you go through the door of the court you are completely at the mercy of what the judge will decide. That might be a decision which is utterly devastating in its effect, on one side or the other. It can be, and surprisingly often is, a decision about which neither party feels particularly happy.

If you do decide to reach an agreement without the court, assistance with negotiating settlements in financial matters is available through organisations like the Family Mediators Association. Professionally trained mediators, who are strictly neutral in their approach, are available to help and advise on what would be a fair settlement in any case. The fees charged involve couples in much less expense than the costs of a court battle. The process is far less of a strain on the emotions than an appearance in court, which most people find a huge ordeal.

If you do reach agreement, the agreement can be made into a court order by consent, without the necessity of anyone actually going to the court to give evidence.

Some orders which the court can make
In divorce proceedings there are several types of order which the court can make. The most common orders are:

1 Maintenance orders
Orders can be made that one spouse makes maintenance or periodical payments to the other (usually the husband to the wife). The payments are normally made on a weekly or monthly basis. They can be ordered for a set period. For example, in the case where

Julie was training to be a bookkeeper (page 32), the court might order Tim to make periodical payments to her for a period of only twelve months.

It is the hope and the aim of the courts that husbands and wives will eventually become financially independent of one another, so that the "meal ticket for life" situation does not arise. But in the case of Doreen and Frank (page 34) we saw that it is not always possible for the court to take the view that someone is capable of achieving financial independence.

If a husband fails to make payments under a court order enforcement proceedings can be taken in the court where the order was made. If the husband is in employment it is possible to obtain an attachment of earnings order to ensure that his employers deduct the amount he should be paying from his wages and then pay it to the wife directly.

If for some reason it is not possible to obtain an attachment of earnings order, a husband who persistently fails to comply with a court order for maintenance could eventually be sent to prison.

Maintenance orders can be varied if there is a change in circumstances. If the husband loses his job he can apply to vary the payments downwards. If the wife, for example, has a part-time job and loses that she can apply for a variation to increase the maintenance order. You will find more information on maintenance, in particular Child Support legislation, in Chapter 9.

2 Lump sum orders
The court can order a husband or a wife to make a payment of a lump sum of money to the other party. This sum can be of any amount, depending upon the assets of the parties in any particular case. This can be ordered in addition to maintenance payments or it can be a final settlement of the financial obligations of the payer.

3 Transfers of property
The court can order a husband or a wife to transfer any property which belongs to that person to the other spouse. This order is most often made when the property to be transferred is the former matrimonial home of the parties. In the particular circumstances of a case, it may be decided by the court that, for example, the wife should have the husband's share of a jointly owned home transferred to her.

The court can also order the transfer of other forms of property, company shares for example.

The powers of the court

From all this you can see that when a marriage breaks down the courts have almost limitless power and discretion to look at the whole picture: the needs of the husband and wife, the overriding necessity to put the welfare of any children of the family first, the assets available by way of income and capital, and the contributions made by each of the parties to the marriage.

Taking these and all the other considerations mentioned into account, the court does the best it can to ensure that the assets of the parties are as fairly divided up between them as possible, bearing in mind of course the overriding concern for any children.

These powers of the court when marriages break down are not, however, available when a non-married relationship breaks down.

Unmarried Couples

Marriage has rather gone out of fashion. In the days of our grandparents, if a man and woman had decided to live openly together in a sexual relationship without getting married, they would have had a hard time of it, particularly the woman. Even in our own parents' time, a couple in that position would have been unusual and would have caused a lot of gossip. But there was quite a bit of hypocrisy in those days too. If a couple had been careful to avoid making their relationship so obvious that it could not be ignored, other people might be prepared to turn a blind eye.

There was also, of course, the double standard. Men were allowed to behave in ways for which women would be condemned. The ultimate disgrace was for an unmarried woman to have a baby. Not only would she suffer the consequences for the rest of her life, her unfortunate and blameless child would be branded for life as well.

The situation is very different today. Large numbers of young couples are choosing to live together without going through a ceremony of marriage. There are many reasons for this. Undoubtedly, one of the main reasons is that fewer people now have any strong religious belief. Also the fact that so many marriages break down today has definitely contributed to the increase in the numbers of couples who choose to live together without marriage.

Many young couples think that they should try living together for a few years, just to see how it works out, rather than marry straightaway. The snag about this is that it seems that marriages between partners who have already been living together for some years are no more likely to survive than those where the partners do not start living together until after the marriage ceremony has taken place.

The sheer expense of getting married puts a lot of people off. The cost of the average wedding is now estimated at £8,000, a great deal more money than most young couples, or their parents, could run to. One enterprising vicar was convinced that the question of cost was at the root of the reluctance of local couples to marry in his church. So he paid for advertising space in local newspapers, and on local radio and TV programmes. In the media he announced that his church was offering a cut-price package deal for marriages. The deal would include fees for the use of the church and the organist, flowers, lighting and caretaking. The bargain package would cost less than a third of what the cost of all this would normally amount to. He really boosted the number of requests for weddings at his church!

Does the law recognise common law marriage?

You often hear people talk about something which they call "common law marriage", when a couple have lived as husband and wife for a certain length of time just as if they had been married. In this situation shouldn't they have exactly the same rights as though they had been through a ceremony of marriage?

Unfortunately for a large number of disillusioned people – usually women – the answer is no. The law does not recognise any such thing as common law marriage. As far as the law is concerned you are either married or you are not, and it does not matter for how long you may have lived as husband and wife, nor does it matter whether everyone you know believed that you were married.

Sometimes even the children of a family believe that their parents are married when in fact they are not. This might not matter very much in some cases but it can have very sad results in others.

CASE STUDY

> When Noel died, he left his "wife" Siobhan and their teenage
> children in the home which he had owned in his sole name. A
> few months after Noel's death Carmel appeared on the doorstep
> and informed the family that she had been Noel's wife before he
> had formed his relationship with Siobhan. They had never been
> divorced and Noel and Siobhan had lived together without getting
> married. Carmel produced a will in which Noel had left everything
> to her. He had never made another will. Had he been divorced and
> later married Siobhan, his marriage would have revoked the old
> will. But in the circumstances, Carmel was entitled to the home
> occupied by the mother and her children.

When you come to think about it, it would be almost impossible
to find a fair test which would establish something like a common
law marriage. How long would the couple have to live together
for common law marriage to be recognised? Would it have to
be a longer period if the couple had not had children together?
What would happen if one or both had already legally married
someone else?

It is difficulties like these that make it unlikely that such "common
law" marriages will ever be granted the set of legal rights which
comes with marriage. So far as children are concerned, that really
does not matter very much today. A non-married parent can have
exactly the same responsibilities and rights as a married parent.
There is more about this in the chapter on parental responsibility
in the Children section of the book. But so far as property rights
are concerned, whether you have been married or not makes all
the difference to what you can expect to get if your relationship
breaks down.

When two people decide to live together as man and wife without
going through a ceremony of marriage, the commitment they make
to one another is usually one of love. At such an exciting and
romantic time the last thing they want to do is plan what will
happen if they split up.

They may have chosen not to get married because they don't
believe in marriage or they are disillusioned with the whole idea of
matrimony. Or perhaps they feel that they want to wait for a time,
to save up to have a lovely wedding day when they can afford it. Or
maybe one would really have liked to get married while the other
does not feel quite so committed. They may tell each other that it
would be better to wait a few years, to see how things work out.

Or one or both may already be married to someone else. For any of these reasons, or maybe for some other reason, they just move in together without getting married, and set up home. No need for meaningless bits of paper, they may think. We know we love one another and that is enough.

But is it? When a relationship like that does last, it may be quite indistinguishable from a loving partnership between two people who have taken vows together in church, chapel, synagogue, temple or register office and who have a marriage certificate to prove it.

It is when the relationship founders that the difference so often becomes all too stark, because the law does not give the protection to unmarried partners that it provides for those who are married. All too often, in a situation where an unmarried relationship breaks down, it is the woman who gets the raw end of the deal.

CASE STUDY

When Tina met Rod they were instantly attracted to one another. They enjoyed the same music, liked one another's friends, shared the same sense of humour. After a few months they realised that they were in love and wanted to live together. Tina was sharing a rented flat with two other girls. Rod was buying his flat on a mortgage. When they decided to live together, the obvious thing to do was for Tina to move into Rod's flat, which she did. They were short of money, so although marriage was discussed they decided to wait for a time and see how things worked out and when they could afford a wedding. As time passed, the subject of getting married just never seemed to come up again.

Both Tina and Rod had well-paid jobs in the computer business. Their earnings were pretty much on a par with each other. It had been agreed that Rod would continue to pay the mortgage and the other outgoings on the flat, including water rates and the bills for gas, electricity and the telephone. Tina would pay for their food, their clothes and their holidays.

Sadly, their relationship did not last. They lived together for ten years. But there came a time when Tina realised that Rod was having an affair with a girl he had met at work. There was a blazing row between them. Tina packed her belongings and left the flat immediately afterwards.

The flat had never been transferred into their joint names. It had simply never occurred to Tina to suggest to Rod that it should be. It was their home, and if she thought about it at all she assumed that, by her contributions over the years in paying for the food, the clothes and the holidays, she would have acquired a fair share in the property. She suggested to Rod that he could raise an extra mortgage to buy out her interest in the flat. Then she could use the

money as a deposit on a flat for herself. She knew that Rod would
have no difficulty in raising the amount she thought she would be
entitled to, on his salary.

But the breakdown of the relationship had been acrimonious.
Rod was not in the mood to agree to anything which Tina
suggested. "It's my flat," he told her. "It's always been my flat. You
have no interest in it. You're not entitled to a penny from me."

Tina was outraged. She went to see a solicitor. She told the
solicitor her story and asked how much the solicitor thought her
interest in Rod's flat would be worth. Unfortunately for Tina, the
answer had to be that Rod was right. The law is very clear on
property rights when people have not been married. Tina had made
no actual payments in money towards the mortgage instalments
or towards improvements made to the flat, and therefore she
had acquired no interest whatsoever in it. "But what about our
agreement – that I would pay for food and holidays and he would
pay the other outgoings?" she asked. "Surely that gives me an
interest?"

The solicitor asked if there had been an agreement between her
and Rod that she should have an interest in the flat if she paid
for their food, clothing and holidays. But there had never been
any discussion between Tina and Rod about the ownership of the
flat. So, sadly for Tina – and for thousands of women, and some
men, who have found themselves in her position – the law could
not help.

CASE STUDY

Flo was another unlucky lady. She met George when she was only
eighteen years old. George was a widower with three very young
children. Flo fell in love with George and moved in to live with
him in the house which he was buying on a mortgage. As the eldest
child was only six years old, there was no question of Flo going
out to work. But she loved children and gladly set about caring
for George's home and family, while he went out to work.

Flo brought up George's children but he and she never married.
They had been living together for over twenty years when George
told her that there was someone else. He told Flo that she would
have to leave, as he intended to invite his new girlfriend to live
with him.

Flo was devastated. Now in her early forties, she had never had
a job outside the home. She had no experience of anything other
than being a wife and mother. She, like Tina, had never worried
about whether she had an interest in the house which had been
her home. She had not expected that her relationship with George
would ever come to an end. It was just like a marriage.

When Flo went to see a solicitor she was given the same bad news.
Her contribution as unpaid housekeeper and mother to someone
else's children had not given her any right to any interest in the
property which had always been in George's sole name, and which

he had purchased before they had met. She had never contributed any money towards the purchase of the home. George had never promised her that she would have an interest in it. They had not been married. So she could not claim that she had acquired any right to a share in it.

Had either Tina been married to Rod, or Flo to George, their situation would have been entirely different. On divorce, the courts have huge powers to make orders about what should happen to property. It would not have mattered in the slightest that Rod's flat was in his sole name or George's house in his. Tina's contributions by paying for food, clothes and holidays would have been taken into consideration, even though she had not made any direct contribution towards the mortgage or improvements to the flat. Flo's contribution in caring for the home and the children would have been recognised, even though she had never been able to contribute financially.

Tina and Flo should serve as awful warnings to anyone thinking of setting up home with someone who is already purchasing a property in his or her sole name. It may be less than romantic, but couples who do not marry should sit down and have a full discussion about what is to happen to any property which is to be their home and which one of them is buying on a mortgage, or already owns.

Ideally, if you are both going to contribute in the way in which married couples usually do – either by pooling your earnings or by one bringing up the children while the other has the job – the property should be legally conveyed into your joint names. The conveyance should set out what your respective interests are to be – whether you are going to share equally or, if not, in what proportions the shares are to be. It really cannot be said often enough that if you are considering living together without getting married you should consult a solicitor if the purchase of any property is involved.

When you buy together
Rod and George were already purchasing their homes when they met the women who moved in with them. But many other young couples who live together without marriage actually decide to purchase a property together in their joint names. So is there any problem with that?

The answer is that, again, it must be kept in mind that cohabitation is not marriage. The law cannot do for unmarried couples what it can do for those who have been legally married. It is absolutely essential if you are thinking about purchasing a property with your partner, and you are not married, that you should talk about what interest each of you is to have in the property you are going to buy. This is because so many joint purchasers have been shocked to discover, when their relationship broke down, that the fact that the property is registered in joint names does not mean that they have automatically acquired equal shares in it.

This is an extremely tricky area of law, even for lawyers. Again, it is of the utmost importance to make sure that you consult your solicitor when you decide to buy a home in your joint names. Make it clear to the solicitor what you have decided your respective interests in the property are to be if your relationship breaks down. This might depend on which of you has paid the deposit or on whether one of you has already been buying the property in his or her sole name.

When you are starting out together in a loving relationship, it probably seems incredible to you that someone you love so much could ever behave unfairly or let you down. Unfortunately, the stark reality is that people are being treated shabbily by ex-lovers every day of the week. Try to make sure that it never happens to you or to someone you care about. Remember, if you are going to live together without getting married, you need to protect yourself by thinking ahead to what might happen if it all goes terribly wrong.

3

THE FUTURE FOR DIVORCE

For some considerable time, there has been growing disquiet among those concerned with the law and also among the general public about the way in which the divorce laws have been working. The continuing emphasis on guilt and innocence in divorce suits, the confrontational stance adopted by some legal advisers, and the speed at which a divorce could be obtained, often giving the partners no opportunity properly to consider the consequences for themselves and their children, were all matters of deep concern. Furthermore, the cost to the country of marriage breakdown, both in financial and in emotional terms, has been escalating alarmingly. A staggering £180 million a year goes on legal aid costs relating to divorce. The additional cost to the NHS by reason of illnesses related to the stress of marital breakdown, to employers by reason of absenteeism through such illness and to the state in financial support given to broken families obviously exceeds even that figure.

It is against this background that the government have been considering possible changes to the divorce law. These are set out in the consultation paper called *Looking to the Future*.

Suggestions for Change

One of the main suggestions being made by the government is that there should really be only the one ground for divorce, that the marriage has broken down irretrievably. The law does say this at the moment, but the need to prove facts such as adultery or unreasonable behaviour carries on the bitterness associated with divorce. So the suggestion is that the only way of proving irretrievable breakdown should be that the parties have been living separately for a specific period of time. This should eliminate all the frustration and acrimony produced by the present system, where the idea of innocence and guilt still exists.

If changes are to be made they will be the first substantial alterations to divorce law for a quarter of a century. The consultation paper has made it clear that the primary aim will be to support the institution of marriage as far as possible. To achieve this, couples thinking about a divorce will be offered expert counselling to help them think about whether there might be any hope of saving their marriages after all. If there is indeed no hope for a marriage, the objective will be to lessen the emotional pain and bitterness for the couple, and above all for any children they may have.

The Lord Chancellor has made various suggestions. One is that the law of divorce should stay as it is. It seems unlikely that there will be a great deal of support for that, in view of all the problems with the present law.

Mediation

One of the main changes being suggested is to focus on mediation, i.e. helping couples to make their own decisions about what should happen so far as children, money and property are concerned, when their marriages have broken down. Much of the distress could be eliminated from divorce if negotiations could be conducted through skilled mediators rather than through lawyers battling it out in court.

The great advantage of mediation is that it helps a couple to negotiate about solutions to their problems rather than fight. Skilled mediators do not tell people what to do, they help them to identify their own problems and discuss them together to find their own solutions to them. Mediation does not have to be just between the partners themselves. It can involve their children, if they are old enough to be consulted. It can involve other people who are part of the picture – new partners for example, or grandparents. It tries to help couples to avoid getting upset about unhappy mistakes which have been made in the past. Instead, they are asked to concentrate on what is to happen in the future, about the proposed divorce, about the children, about money, about homes.

In this way it is hoped that acrimony can be reduced and emotional stresses lessened, not only for the husband and wife but, even more crucially, for their children. When a couple have found their own solutions to their problems through mediation each is more likely to feel that there has been a satisfactory outcome. Their children will be reassured to be told that the parents have been able to make their own decisions about all the important changes which will have to take place.

Possible problems

The down side, of course, is that if the mediator is not sufficiently skilled the partners may feel that pressure is being exerted on them to reach a particular solution. Or if one partner is weaker or less able to speak up than the other it could happen that the stronger partner will override him or her. This could mean that the weaker partner feels he or she has been bullied or browbeaten into accepting the other's terms. It also has to be said that, since mediation is a comparatively new approach in divorce, there has not yet been a great deal of research to provide hard evidence about its effectiveness and the long-term results, although so far the information about it is encouraging.

Should every divorcing couple have to go to mediation?

It has been suggested that every couple thinking about getting a divorce should be forced to attend mediation sessions. However, it is unlikely that this will happen. Some couples are able to arrange their own affairs without seeking any professional help. It would obviously be quite wrong for the law to insist that couples should be forced to talk about their problems to an outsider if they can reach their own solutions without doing so. What will probably happen is that every couple thinking about a divorce will be given information about services of mediation which are available, so that they can decide for themselves whether they wish to make use of them.

It is suggested that for someone thinking about getting a divorce there should be a personal interview, during which information about the legal procedures and the consequences of divorce would be given face to face. An information pack would also be provided. At that early stage advice would be given about marriage guidance to enable the couple to think carefully about whether there might be any possibility of saving their marriage. Information would also be given about the likely costs of court proceedings and of mediation.

If there is support for this idea, it has not yet been decided who would conduct these interviews. Possible candidates might be court welfare officers, mediators or trained personnel in some independent organisation which has not yet been set up.

Another important suggestion is that there should always be a "breathing space" period between that initial interview and the actual time when a divorce could be granted. The length of that breathing space has yet to be decided, but it would certainly ensure that couples had some time to think about what divorcing would actually mean, to themselves and to their children, before taking any final step. If there is really no hope at all for the marriage, the breathing space would still give time for the couple to negotiate agreements about children, money and homes.

These are all just suggestions at the moment. But everyone connected with the law of divorce is agreed that some changes will have to be made. Many of the suggestions being made do seem to mean that there will be considerable improvements to the present situation.

What is essential is that sufficient funds should be made available for the provision of adequate training for suitably qualified professionals. There has been a suggestion that failure to achieve a mediated settlement might mean that legal aid could be denied to couples who might need the advice of lawyers. This could obviously produce very unfair results, particularly where one partner is in a financial position to afford a lawyer and the other is not.

II

Children

4

HOW THE LAW
HAS CHANGED

In an ideal world, the two most important people in the life of any child should be his or her mother and father. Unfortunately, today more and more children are being brought up by one parent alone, by a parent and a step-parent, or even without either of their parents, in the care of a local authority.

The law has had to become involved more often with children, partly as a result of the changing patterns in family life, and partly because of the numbers of children who have been suffering from the most appalling cruelty through neglect or emotional or physical abuse of some sort. It is becoming impossible to open a newspaper without reading details of yet another case where a child has suffered at the hands of the adults who should be giving him protection and love.

Why Did the Law Have to Change?

Until 1989, when the Children Act was passed, the law concerning children was in a complete shambles. Cases about the same child could be brought to court in many different ways. It could and did happen that there were cases going on about the same child in two or three different courts during the same period of time. It was a frequent complaint that children were being seriously emotionally damaged by delayed cases. To a small child a few months can seem an eternity. The younger the child, the more irreversible the damage which could be done by delay.

We are all aware of the tragic cases where small children suffer the most terrible injuries at the hands of violent parents or step-parents, sometimes even resulting in death. Cases like these underlined the need to tighten up the system for protecting children and for stepping in quickly where there is a real suspicion that a child might be being abused in some way.

Children of divorce

Divorce was another area where children could be unnecessarily hurt. It is devastating enough for a child when his or her parents decide they no longer love one another, but the rules laid down in divorce cases meant that there could be additional tensions imposed on the family. For example, even in a case where the parents had come to a sensible agreement between themselves about with which parent the children should live and about how often they should have contact with the other parent, the court still had to make an order. It was almost as though the law took the view that if your marriage had broken down you could not be trusted to make decisions about your own children.

If the parents could not agree, they had to battle in court over who should have custody of the children and how much access the other parent should have. Custody came to be looked on almost as ownership of a child. No matter how hard the courts tried to make it clear that even if one parent had legal custody the other was still just as much of a parent, the message was definitely not getting through. Warring parents refused to look on a custody order as anything but a matter of winning or losing. All too often, the parent who got the custody order would then behave as though it meant that the other parent could be excluded from the child's life as far as possible. Every request for access would mean a further skirmish in the battle, in many cases another fight in court. And once again the real casualties would be the children.

The child's voice

Children themselves had very little, if any, say in decision-making about what should happen to them. Until fairly recently as far as the law was concerned, children were, of course, children until they reached the age of eighteen. Decisions were made over their heads, without anyone giving any particular thought to their age or maturity, or considering that they might have a right to a say in the decision-making process.

Professionals concerned with children – lawyers, social workers and child psychologists among them – recognised the problems. Why should parents not be given more responsibility for deciding what should happen to their own children? Why should the court have to become involved if they can reach agreement between themselves? Why should the children themselves, depending on their age and understanding, not be given a real voice when what was to happen to them was being discussed?

In 1989 the Children Act was passed in an effort to tackle these problems and others. For the first time all the law relating to children had been brought together. "Custody" and "access", old-fashioned legal words which had become so emotive, were to be replaced by the more neutral terms "residence" and "contact".

Within living memory, children were very much the property of their parents. The parents might be good, caring and loving or bad, neglectful and abusive of their children. It was only in the most extreme cases of cruelty that the law would interfere with the way in which children were treated by their carers. However, the changing pattern of adult relationships, and in particular the breakdown of so many married and unmarried partnerships, has been a major factor in the law becoming increasingly involved with children. One out of every five children in this country is being brought up by a single parent. Countless numbers of children are being brought up in homes where one of the parental figures is not their natural parent.

Laws have had to be made relating to disputes between parents and others about where and with whom children should live, and with whom and in what circumstances they should have contact. Laws have had to be made to deal with financial support for the carers of children.

One of the more horrific aspects of life in our society today is that so many children suffer from abuse and neglect. Abuse can be physical or emotional. Over the last twenty years the problem of abuse of children appears to have increased, particularly with regard to sexual abuse. Whatever the reasons for this, and they are many and complex, the law has had to intervene to try to protect children.

Family breakdown, coupled with the need to protect children from abuse and neglect, has meant that a growing number of children have had to be cared for away from their own families. Laws have had to be made about how children should be looked after when, for some reason, their own families cannot cope, and they need to be fostered, adopted or put into local authority care. (For further information on this see Chapters 10 and 11.)

Over the last hundred years the emphasis has completely shifted from parental *rights* to parental *responsibility*. One of the most important things to realise about parental responsibility is that it can be shared equally by the mother and the father, even after they have separated or been divorced. In the past, if one parent had been granted a custody order, the other parent often felt excluded from the child's life, or at best marginalised.

Custody is an outdated notion. Since the law relating to children was reformed, the parent with whom the child will be living is given a residence order. If the parents agree about where the child should live there is no need for the court to make any order at all.

CASE STUDY

William's mother has obtained a residence order from the court which says that he is to live with her. William's father has been granted a contact order which sets out the periods which William will spend with him. But these orders do not in any way lessen the parental responsibility of William's father who can exercise his parental responsibility in any way he thinks best in William's interests whenever William is visiting him.

Both parents should feel that each has an equal opportunity to take part in decision-making about the upbringing of their child and that they are equally responsible for their child, whoever happens to have the residence order. Parental responsibility enables a parent to take part in decisions about the important things which are to happen in the child's life.

In the past, because children were looked on as little more than the possessions of their parents, the law tended to enforce the "rights" of parents over the children. In fact, not all that long ago, it was only the father who had rights; the mother had none at all. For example, it was not uncommon for a mother who had been found to have committed adultery to be refused any future contact with her child by the court. But if mothers were given no rights over their children, the children were in an even worse position.

Pity poor Harriet, whose mother had left her father for very good reasons in 1878. The father took Harriet and her brothers and sisters away from their mother with the full approval of the court. The eldest child was twelve years old. The father could not look after them himself so he boarded them out with "clergymen and other persons . . . in many and various places". He permitted their mother to visit them only once every month, and he insisted that any letters written to the mother by the children and by the mother to the children had to be censored.

Harriet must have been a brave girl. When she was sixteen she wrote to the judge and asked him to allow her to live with her mother. If she could not live with her, would the judge allow Harriet to spend a holiday with her? Her letter was a sad one. "Father has no place to take me to, and with one exception has never spent a vacation with us over four years. I am almost always among strangers. I am longing to see some of my relations," she wrote.

But when her request came to be considered by the court, it was decided that the court had no power to interfere with the legal right of a father to have absolute control over his children and to decide where they should live and who they should see.

Contrast what happened to poor Harriet and her mother with what happened almost exactly a hundred years later, when Mrs Victoria Gillick, the mother of five girls, attempted to persuade a court that advice on contraception should not be given to her daughters while they were under the age of sixteen, unless she as their mother had agreed that such advice could be given.

The House of Lords decided that Mrs Gillick did not have complete control over her children. It said that the rights of a parent come from the parent's duty to protect the child. But the child has rights too. As a child grew older and more intelligent and mature, the rights of the child increased. In other words, a child who is old enough and intelligent enough to understand what is to be decided and what the consequences of a decision will be, must be allowed to make his or her own choice. As the child grows in maturity and intelligence so the right of the parents to make decisions about the child gradually dwindle away. Mrs Gillick's right to choose whether or not her child could have certain medical advice would come to an end if and when each child was intelligent enough to understand what the choice was and what the consequences were likely to be. So this case paved the way for the child's right to a voice in decisions to be made about him or her by the courts.

There is a checklist for the court which sets out the matters which have to be considered in any case about children. The full checklist is given later in this chapter. But what is interesting is that the very first item for the court to consider which is set out in the checklist is "the ascertainable wishes and feelings of the child . . . considered in the light of (his or her) age and understanding".

Family lawyers can tell you from experience that the wishes and feelings of almost every child involved in any court proceedings where parents are in conflict are sadly predictable. Occasionally, in special circumstances, a judge will agree to see the children during a case where their future is under discussion. This does not happen very often because the judge will usually have the assistance of a report from the court welfare officer. When a judge decides to see them, the children will be brought to a private room, away from the court itself. The argument between the parents may be about with which of them the children are to live. The judge will talk to the children without either parent or their legal representatives being in the room.

The judge then comes back into court, having talked to the children, to explain to the parents what the children have said. Almost always the judge will say that the children have said that they want only that their mother and father should live together again, without any arguments. The judge will point out that this is one order which the court cannot make. He or she will then go on to do the best that can be done if the parents have decided that they cannot go on together and cannot even agree about what should happen to their children.

Will a court always order what the children want?

Great importance is now given to the wishes and feelings of children, but what a child wants cannot always be the end of the matter. For example, there was a recent case where a child of twelve was described by a judge as "fixed and determined" in her desire to live with her father. But the judge then went on to say that the child was too young to carry the burden of decisions about her own future. He said that she must be told, with appropriate sympathy and firmness, that the decision and the responsibility for it had to be made for her. She would be sad, the judge thought, but she must be helped to make the best of it.

This does not mean that every twelve-year-old would be considered too young to make decisions. For example, the wishes of a twelve-year-old about whether or not to have contact with someone might be quite decisive. Children do mature at different rates and one girl of twelve may be quite childish still, while her friend of exactly the same age might be quite mature and responsible. The court tries to assess the intelligence and understanding of the individual child in each case, rather than taking some arbitrary rule of thumb based on age alone.

Does the court have to make an order about a child?

As a matter of fact the court need not make any order at all if it considers that this would be better for the child concerned. This "leave well alone" idea is a new one. Before the Children Act was passed an order would always be made by the court if an application about a child had been made. The order would be made even if the case had been settled by agreement. In every divorce case where there were children of the family the court had to make custody and access orders even if there was no dispute about what should happen. This minimised the responsibility of the parents. The new approach underlines the fact that it is the parents who have the primary responsibility where decisions have to be made about the future of their children.

From the child's point of view, how much happier it will make him or her to be told that his mother and father have taken the decision about what is to happen together, rather than becoming aware that an almighty court battle is taking place, with an order having to be made which will leave one parent a "winner" and the other a "loser".

There are four separate and equally important things which any judge must bear in mind when dealing with a case concerning a child:

(a) the welfare of the child is paramount in deciding all questions about the child;
(b) delay in deciding any question about a child's upbringing is likely to prejudice the child's welfare;
(c) there is a checklist (see below) of matters to which the court has to pay particular attention;
(d) the court should not make an order unless to do so is considered better for the child than making no order.

The checklist

The court has to pay particular attention to the following matters, set out in the Act and described as "the checklist":

(a) the ascertainable wishes and feelings of the child concerned (considered in the light of his age and understanding);
(b) the physical, emotional and educational needs of the child;
(c) the likely effect upon the child of any change in the circumstances of the child;
(d) the age, sex and background of the child and any other characteristics of the child which the court considers relevant;
(e) any harm which the child has suffered or which the child may be at risk of suffering;
(f) how capable each of the child's parents, and any other person in relation to whom the court considers the question to be relevant, is of meeting his needs;
(g) the range of powers available to the court under the Act in the proceedings before it.

Welfare

Some of these matters need a little further explanation. What exactly is "welfare", for example?

One judge has said this: "Welfare is an all-encompassing word. It includes material welfare, both in the sense of adequacy of resources to provide a pleasant home and a comfortable standard of living and in the sense of adequacy of care to ensure that good health and due personal pride are maintained. However, while material considerations have their place they are secondary matters.

"More important are the stability and security, the loving and understanding care and guidance, the warm and compassionate relationships, that are essential for the full development of the child's own character, personality and talents."

It would be hard to find a better way of describing the welfare principle.

Delay

Most parents would wholeheartedly agree that delay in deciding some dispute about a child, with which of them the child is to live for example, can have very serious effects on the child, quite apart from the worry, disappointment and frustration experienced by the parents.

In the past, cases would often drag on for weeks, months, even years. Solicitors often have very heavy caseloads. Some solicitors are less efficient than others. It could and did happen that cases concerning children were put on the back burner because other matters seemed more urgent or important.

To parents or other concerned people, delay in deciding some question about a child can be infuriating. There were many cases in which the single factor of delay really forced the court into a decision which would not have been taken if the matter could have come before the court reasonably promptly.

CASE STUDY

> Four-year-old Billy had been placed with long-term foster parents for a year or two before the application by his parents to have him returned came to court. The court was faced with the problem that the parents, who might otherwise have been able to have Billy returned to them, were now almost strangers as far as he was concerned. To uproot him from the family he viewed as his own would have caused great and possibly irreparable harm. So the court, in Billy's interests, would have to refuse the parents' application.

Cases like Billy's resulted in the new system under the Children Act. This requires the court to make orders to keep cases moving along, to set dates by which certain procedures should be carried out, and to make sure that solicitors have a timetable which they must be careful to keep.

How is the act working?

The many new provisions of the Children Act have only been in force for a relatively short time. Obviously, there have been teething troubles but it certainly has achieved some of its objectives. Parents are thinking more about responsibility than their "rights". Children's voices are being heard. Cases about children are, on the whole, coming to court faster.

Few, if any, family lawyers would want to go back to the situation before the Act came into force.

5

PARENTAL RESPONSIBILITY

Parental "rights" have disappeared and have been replaced by what the law calls parental responsibility, i.e. the obligations of any parent to care for his or her own child. What are these responsibilities of parenthood?

When you come to think about it, the responsibilities of a parent are actually changing all the time, as the child develops. It would be difficult if not impossible to compile a comprehensive list of them because the contents of the list would change from month to month and from year to year as the child grew up. The parents of a newborn baby have quite different responsibilities from those which they have when their baby has become a teenager. It might be possible to list all the responsibilities of a parent at one particular stage in a child's life, but the responsibilities on that list would be the ones for that stage and would constantly have to be changed as the child became more independent and more able to take decisions for itself. And you can't just rely on the child's age – the responsibilities on you as a parent at a particular point in time will depend on all kinds of variable factors – no child develops at exactly the same rate and in exactly the same ways as any other.

So it is difficult to attempt to define exactly what parental responsibility is. I suppose the best definition is that it includes a duty to do whatever seems to be in the best interests of your child at whatever stage he or she is in life.

Who Has Parental Responsibility?

When the mother and father of a child are married to each other at the date of the child's birth, each will automatically have parental responsibility for that child. The parental responsibility will not be taken from one or the other parent as a result of divorce or separation. If you or your ex have been given custody of a child before the 1989 Children Act that does not mean that your ex has lost his or her parental responsibility.

If a mother and father are not married at the date of the child's birth, but were married at any time during the period when the mother was carrying the child, the father still gets parental responsibility on the birth of the child. Even if the baby was the result of artificial insemination the position would still be the same.

CASE STUDY

> Sophie's parents are Andrew and Jill. When Sophie was conceived Andrew and Jill were married. Sadly, they divorced two months before Sophie's birth. Andrew and Jill will both have parental responsibility for Sophie, even though they had ceased to be married before she was born.

CASE STUDY

> Gary and Sue have a son called Michael. When Michael was conceived Gary and Sue were not married to one another, but they married during Sue's pregnancy. Both Sue and Gary automatically acquired parental responsibility when Michael was born.

If you are an unmarried father can you get parental responsibility?

CASE STUDY

> Richard and Jane have never been married. They have a daughter, Elizabeth. Jane, as the mother, acquired immediate parental responsibility when Elizabeth was born. Richard, like many unmarried fathers, wants to play a full part in the life of his little girl, even though he and her mother are not married. How can he get parental responsibility for Elizabeth?

There are a number of ways in which fathers like Richard can acquire parental responsibility:

(a) If Jane agrees that Richard should have all the legal responsibilities of a father, she can enter into a formal agreement with him that he should have parental responsibility. As a result of that formal agreement, Richard will acquire parental responsibility for Elizabeth without any necessity to go to court to ask for an order.

(b) If a court had already granted Richard custody or care and control over Elizabeth under the old law, that order would have given him parental responsibility.

(c) If Richard has not been granted an order for custody or care and control of Elizabeth under the old law, and if Jane does not agree that he should have parental responsibility, Richard can apply to the court for a parental responsibility order.

(d) Richard might think that it would be in Elizabeth's best interests to live with him rather than with her mother. In those circumstances, he could apply for a residence order (which used to be called a custody order). If the court decided to grant him a residence order, a parental responsibility order would also be made.

How does the court decide about giving parental responsibility?

The court always has to think about what would be in the best interests of the child concerned. So Richard's application for a parental responsibility order will be considered in the light of what would be in Elizabeth's best interests. Elizabeth's own wishes and feelings will be taken into account, if she is old enough to understand what her father's application means. Her physical, emotional and educational needs will also be considered, as will the likely effect on her of any order made as a result of Richard's application. Her age, sex and background will be relevant. There may be other things about her which the court will consider relevant too. The court must also consider whether Elizabeth has suffered or is likely to suffer any harm as a result of Richard's application or of any order which might be made.

For example, suppose that Richard had another daughter whom he had seriously abused. The court would probably decide that there could be a risk that he would similarly abuse Elizabeth. In those circumstances, it would probably refuse to grant the parental responsibility order.

It is very likely that the court would request the help of a court welfare officer before making a decision about Richard's application. The welfare officer would make enquiries and talk to everyone concerned in order to be able to provide the judge with information about Elizabeth and her parents and background. What a court welfare officer does is fully explained in Chapter 8.

Some matters which will be important when the court considers a father's application are:

(a) the degree of commitment which the father has shown towards the child;
(b) the degree of attachment which exists between the father and the child;
(c) the father's reasons for applying for the order.

For example, if Richard had shown little or no real interest in Elizabeth up until the time when he made his application to the court, it is unlikely that the court would be prepared to make a parental responsibility order in his favour.

Again, if Elizabeth has had contact with Richard but without becoming fond of him, Richard's case for a parental responsibility order might be a weak one. However, it has to be said that if Elizabeth's mother Jane has consistently obstructed contact so that there has been no possibility of Elizabeth forming an attachment to Richard, his application might still succeed if he could show that it would be in Elizabeth's interests to form a relationship with him.

Richard's reasons for applying for the order will be very important. It is not unknown, unfortunately, for a father to make an application about a child simply in order to interfere in the life of the mother or to avenge himself for some former hurt. If the court were to take the view that Richard had some such motivation, this would be likely to be fatal to his application.

In Richard's case, as with every other case where a parent makes an application about a child, his interests as a father will not override what the court considers to be in the best interests of Elizabeth. You might think that this was so obviously the correct approach that the courts of any civilised country would take the same view.

Surprisingly, not all legal systems put the interests of the child first.

CASE STUDY

In a recent American case, for example, a little girl, adopted as a baby was taken away at age two and a half from the only parents she had ever really known. Sobbing for her "mommy", she was strapped into a child's seat in her natural father's car and driven off. That father was a stranger so far as the child was concerned, but his rights were allowed to predominate.

TV cameras recorded the child's distress and bewilderment. Her mother, when agreeing to the adoption, had lied about the identity of the father. That resulted in a legal situation where the father's "rights" were the most important consideration, whatever the resultant trauma to a toddler might be.

But putting the child's interests first does not mean that decisions about giving parental responsibility, to someone like Richard for example, are easy ones for the court to make.

The problems for the court

CASE STUDY

Carl was four years old. His parents had separated when he was three months old. His father had made no attempt to keep in contact with him, he had paid no maintenance for him nor had he ever sent presents, cards or letters at times like birthdays or Christmas. Eventually, however, his father had applied for access (now called contact) with Carl.

By the time his father's application came before the court, Carl was three and a half. The first judge granted access initially to take place in the presence of a court welfare officer. Carl's mother appealed. She had remarried and made a new life for herself and her son. She viewed the prospect of Carl's introduction to his father as nothing less than a disaster.

So far as Carl himself was concerned, he believed that his mother's new husband was his daddy. His mother's anxiety about his father's proposed entry into Carl's life was such that it was bound to be sensed by Carl. The relationship between Carl's mother and his stepfather would also be placed under strain. That strain would inevitably affect Carl himself.

The appeal judge asked himself what good the father could do Carl. The answer was none. What harm could he do him? The answer was possibly a great deal. To take Carl to meet his father who was a stranger to him seemed a horrifying idea.

The court went on to talk about the pain and anguish which would be caused to Carl's mother, her parents and her second husband by the introduction of Carl to his father.

The test was said to be whether starting access now, after this long lapse of time, would be of any positive benefit to Carl.

All three of the judges who heard the appeal understood that the judge who made the access order had been guided by the principle that children ought to know their fathers. While agreeing with that principle in theory, they considered that the circumstances of that particular little boy were such that his interests overrode the principle.

Although this particular case was decided before the Children Act was passed, the approach taken by the appeal judges in the case would still serve as a guideline to judges considering applications for parental responsibility by fathers who had not had contact with their children for a long time.

It must be stressed that every case depends upon its own facts. It is certainly not true that contact or a parental responsibility order will always be refused where there has been a gap in contact between father and child. Nor will it invariably be refused when the mother has made a new relationship. But these factors will undoubtedly be given weight when the court has to make a decision about introducing an unknown father into the life of his child, and particularly where the child has no idea that he has any father but the one who lives with his mother.

Had the little American girl been a child adopted in this country, it is unlikely that a judge would have made an order which had the effect of uprooting her from adoptive parents, with whom she was happy and settled, to place her in the care of the father whom she did not know.

Divorced or separated parents

Where parents who have been married are separated or divorced each of them will continue to have parental responsibility. This means that a parent who does not have a child living with him or her should still be treated as a parent by, for example, the child's school. In the past, when a custody order had been made in favour of one parent, head teachers of the children's schools all too frequently behaved as though the children had only one parent.

In such situations the parent who did not have care and control would receive no copies of school reports and no invitations to parents' evenings or school functions. Not every school took this line, of course, but it was certainly not uncommon.

Any parent who was marginalised by the child's school in this way was bound to feel upset and frustration. The Law Commission, which considered the concept of parental responsibility prior to the Children Act, emphasised in its report that a parent who does not have the child with him or her should still be regarded in law as a parent. It was specifically pointed out that such parents should be treated as parents by schools and given information and an opportunity to take part in the education of their children.

Some head teachers would make the excuse that because they were providing the custodial parent with reports and information, they expected that parent to pass everything on to the other parent. In an ideal world, one might expect that sort of co-operation between parents no longer living together. Unfortunately, in the real world, the head teachers were often being over-optimistic.

Exercising parental responsibility

Parental responsibility can be exercised independently by a parent when the child is in his care, whether or not that parent has a residence order. However, there are certain limitations to this and it can be a tricky area.

CASE STUDY

> Sarah and Tom are the divorced parents of Luke. A residence order has been made in favour of Sarah. Luke attends a school in the area of his home with Sarah. The school does not accept a certain style of haircut and will exclude any boy with that hairstyle.
>
> Luke is having weekend staying contact with Tom. Can Tom decide to excercise his parental responsibility by having Luke's hair cut in the style forbidden by the school?
>
> This can be seen as an example of an exercise of parental responsibility by Tom which would be incompatible with the court order that Luke reside with his mother. Consequently, it would not be appropriate for Tom to exercise his parental responsibility in this way. Not many fathers would want to do something likely to have their child excluded from school, so it is to be hoped that this situation would not arise too frequently!
>
> But suppose, during that same weekend, Tom decided to take Luke to a sporting event of which he knew Sarah would disapprove? It would probably be a perfectly proper exercise of Tom's parental responsibility for him to take the decision to bring Luke to the event, even though aware of Sarah's disapproval.

Again, these are examples only. For the sake of Luke's peace of mind, one would hope that Tom and Sarah could reach some agreement about the sporting event to enable Luke to enjoy it without any feeling of guilt about upsetting his mother.

There are some aspects of a child's life which are so fundamentally important that a parent with parental responsibility cannot take a decision about them without the agreement of the other parent with responsibility. For example, whether a child should have an operation or not would usually be a matter for both parents, unless it was an emergency situation. What school a child should attend is also a question which should be jointly decided by both parents. When parents cannot agree on an issue of this kind, either of them can apply to the court for a judge to make a decision. A parent cannot take a child out of the country permanently without the consent of the other parent, and the consent of each parent with responsibility would be required before an adoption order is made in respect of a child.

When someone else acquires parental responsibility

Step-parents
What happens if Sarah remarries and she and her new husband Charles obtain residence orders in respect of Luke? Charles acquires parental responsibility for Luke because of the residence order, but Tom does not lose his parental responsibility. This means that more than two parents can have parental responsibility for the same child.

Children in care
When a care order is made in respect of a child, or when an emergency protection order is taken out, parental responsibility is conferred on the local authority. But the natural parents with parental responsibility do not lose it as a result of a care order or emergency protection order although they will be limited in what they can do.

Adoption
An adoption order confers parental responsibility on the adoptive parent or parents. It terminates the parental responsibility of the natural parents. Adoption will be considered in detail in Chapter 10. NB: Foster parents do not acquire parental responsibility.

Guardians appointed by the court

The court can appoint someone as the guardian of a child, when the parent hasn't done so, in two situations:

(a) Michael's parents are dead so no one has parental responsibility for him. The court can appoint a guardian for Michael who will be given parental responsibility on his or her appointment;
(b) Jennifer lived with her mother Patricia, who had been granted a residence order. Jennifer's father had taken no interest in her for several years. Sadly, Patricia has died of cancer. The court can appoint a guardian for Jennifer and the guardian will have parental responsibility.

It seems that any relative or family friend could apply to be appointed the guardian of a child for whom no one has parental responsibility. In theory, it would appear that a child could apply to the court for a guardian to be appointed if the child is of sufficient maturity to understand the application.

A guardian who is appointed by the court to have parental responsibility for a child should not be confused with a Guardian ad Litem, someone appointed by the court to represent a child in proceedings before the court. The responsibilities of Guardians ad Litem are limited and will be considered in more detail in another chapter.

Guardians appointed by parents

A parent with parental responsibility can appoint a guardian to replace him or her in the event of death. However, if the parent who makes the appointment does not have a residence order, the appointment will not take effect unless and until the parent with the residence order dies too.

Anyone with parental responsibility can appoint someone to be a child's guardian in the event of death. Before the Children Act a parent could only appoint a guardian by executing a legal document called a deed, or by making a will. But it is now sufficient if the appointment is made in writing, is dated and is signed by the person making it.

All parents should think seriously about what they would wish to happen to their children in the event of their death. If you choose a guardian for your children you must, of course, consult that person about whether he or she would be willing to accept the responsibility. Once you have chosen the guardian there is no need to do anything other than record your wish in writing, date it and sign it.

If you are making a will – and everyone should – the appointment of the guardian could be included in that.

When does parental responsibility end?

All parental responsibility ends when the child is eighteen years old. Where the child's parents have never been married and the father has acquired parental responsibility by means of a court order or through the formal consent of the mother, the order or agreement ends automatically once the child reaches the age of eighteen.

The court can also make an order that parental responsibility should end, if it has been acquired by court order or by agreement. An order terminating parental responsibility in such a case can be made on the application of someone with parental responsibility for the child (which will include the father himself). An order terminating parental responsibility can also be made on the application of the child, with the permission of the court. As with any application made by a child, the court will first have to satisfy itself that the child has sufficient understanding to make the application.

Some useful addresses are listed on pp 82–84.

6

WHAT SHOULD WE DO ABOUT THE CHILDREN?

When parents split up, their children are in the front line. If the children are of an age where they still need parental care the first question to be answered is where and with whom they are going to live. Tied up with that decision are the questions about how often and for how long they will see the parent with whom they are not living.

Any breakdown in a relationship is going to be traumatic for the couple concerned. If they have been sufficiently committed to one another to have children, it is almost inevitable that the trauma of the breakdown will be correspondingly greater. Far too often children get caught in the crossfire because parents are too occupied with their own feelings of hurt and rejection to think clearly.

No loving parent would willingly inflict emotional pain on a child. But when coping with the turmoil of separation and loss a parent can be blinded to what should be obvious.

Divorce and Separation: Children Have a Right to Know

Children, even very young children, are only too aware of any tension in the relationship between their parents. The story is told of the couple who resolved that their small son and daughter would never be given a hint of any disagreement between them. When they were irritated with one another they took particular care to be even more polite than usual. They prided themselves on their success in concealing their quarrels until the day when they had to use physical force to separate their squabbling children. The little boy pointed at his sister and said accusingly, "She called me *darling* first!"

That story illustrates precisely what so often happens. Parents may believe that their children have no idea that there are any problems between them. But it is in fact rare for children of a foundering relationship not to realise that one or other of their parents is unhappy or that something is wrong.

Some parents find the temptation to enlist the sympathy of the children irresistible. But most children love their parents equally. Children certainly need both parents. The fact that the parental relationship has broken down should not mean that they lose out any more than they must.

Parents who have decided to separate should try to explain to their children exactly what is happening. If at all possible they should explain to the children together. The words they use will obviously depend upon the ages of the children, but even the smallest children deserve to be given some explanation which they can understand.

Child psychiatrists who have made a study of the children of divorced or separated parents have come up with some surprising conclusions. For example, they have discovered that children often believe that the breakdown of their parents' relationship is somehow their fault. It needs to be carefully explained to a child that adults do stop loving one another sometimes. Equally, it should be emphasised that both parents still love the child and will not stop doing so whatever happens.

Child experts have also found that, if a parent leaves home and there is no careful explanation given to small children, they will worry desperately about the possibility that the parent who is still there will vanish too. The child's reasoning is: if Daddy can go away, so might Mummy. Who will look after me then?

That might seem laughable to an adult. But for the child who does not understand what has happened or why, and to whom no one attempts to explain what has happened, the logic is remorseless.

Small children can feel great anxiety about the parent who leaves. Where will he or she sleep? Who will cook their meals? If there is no discussion about the parents' plans a child may suffer acute and quite unnecessary concern, and this will be in addition to the unavoidable distress caused by the breakdown itself. To see for itself where the absent parent will be living helps the child to come to terms with the new situation.

Some parents feel that talking to their children about the breakdown of their relationship is simply too difficult. But if the children are given no explanation of what is happening in their lives they are likely to be very frightened and confused.

Fortunately, there are now many organisations which are able to help with counselling for parents at times like this. This counselling is called "conciliation" but parents should not be put off by this word. It is often thought to mean "reconciliation" – in other words attempts to patch up a failed relationship. Conciliation recognises that the relationship has broken down. Counsellors work with the parents to find the best solutions to the practical problems thrown up by the breakdown. There is a list of helpful organisations at the end of this chapter. Conciliation through the courts will be discussed more fully in the next chapter.

Custody, Care and Control, and Access

Before the Children Act came into force in 1991 most people were familiar with the ideas of custody, care and control, and access. Parents could have a joint custody order, which gave care and control to one or other of them. Joint custody orders were not all that common, since the court had to be convinced that the parents could work together harmoniously for the good of a child before such an order could be made. More usual were orders which gave sole custody, care and control to one parent.

In either case, the parent who did not have care and control could be granted access – visiting access or staying (overnight) access, or both. In rare cases, a parent would not be given access, or would have access limited to sending letters, cards and gifts.

Custody, care and control were emotive words. The non-custodial parent frequently felt excluded from a child's life. The word "access" appeared to imply that the child somehow "belonged" to the parent who had care and control. The word "custody" appeared to confirm that idea.

The mere fact that whenever a divorce took place there had to be a court order about what should happen to the children often gave rise to difficulties where there should have been none. For example, it was not unusual for separating parents to be in complete agreement about what should happen in relation to their children. But the court still had to intervene by making an order, even though it would be expressed to be "by consent".

There was always some confusion about the extent of the right of the parent who did not have custody to be consulted about important decisions in the life of a child – whether or not the child should have some operation in hospital, for example, or which school should be chosen or which religion the child should be taught. Where parents were not on the best of terms following a split, the tendency might be for the custodial parent to make all the decisions without consulting the other parent at all. This sort of thing would inevitably upset the other parent – and, of course, the child! A parent like this was, unconsciously no doubt, using the child as a weapon in an ongoing conflict with the other parent.

The courts tried to give guidance about this and insisted that a custody order did not give the custodial parent absolute rights over all decision-making about the child. Attempts were sometimes made to overcome the difficulty by granting joint custody orders, in order to emphasise that both parents shared responsibility. However, most judges would only agree to make a joint custody order if they could be satisfied that the parents were able to relate to one another reasonably and to make decisions together. This meant that in the cases where there was most acrimony it was more likely that a sole custody order would be made, giving that parent the power to use the child as a weapon against the other.

It was in order to bring parents back to the realisation that each has equal responsibility for his or her child that custody orders were abolished to be replaced by the – neutral – residence orders.

The old orders still exist, side by side with the new residence and contact orders. Where orders were made before the Children Act came into force, they remain as custody, care and control, and access orders unless or until they are varied by the court on the application of either parent, or even by the child concerned.

New words for old?

Child psychiatrists and other experts agree that the children with separated parents each of whom encourages them to love the other parent, survive the breakdown of their parents' relationship best.

Laws cannot be passed to compel parents to be nice to one another, to put their own hurts aside and to encourage their children to love the parent who may have behaved badly as a partner. But it was realised that the orders which were being made before the Children Act were actually working against parental co-operation. Parents thought of themselves as being "winners" or "losers" when it came to orders relating to children. The parent with care and control had won. The parent with access had lost.

The thinking behind the Children Act was to try to avoid this kind of unnecessary emotional distress for parents, as far as possible. The emphasis is now placed firmly on the idea of parental responsibility. Each parent has equal parental responsibility, whenever the child is with him or her. The very words "custody" and "access" had become loaded with emotive overtones. It was decided that the Act should do away with them.

The choices for the court

The court now has three choices when faced with the problem of what should happen to the children on the breakdown of a marriage:

1   To make no order at all:
This is now the preferred option and one which was simply not open to the court prior to the Children Act. It underlines the fact that each parent has responsibility for the child. The parents are obviously the best people to make decisions about their child. If they can do so, it should be left to them and the court should not intervene. Children themselves will be much happier if they feel that their parents have come to a joint decision about what is to happen to them.

For these reasons parents are very much encouraged by the law to make their own decisions if at all possible. Many agencies have been set up to try to help parents to discuss the future arrangements for their children and to reach an amicable and mutually agreed plan. The court's own conciliation process, which will be discussed in Chapter 7, is another area where help may be found.

2   To make a residence order in favour of one parent and a contact order in favour of the other:
Unfortunately, where parents cannot agree, it has to be admitted that this kind of order will all too frequently be seen by parents in

the old winning/losing terms. The mere change of wording seldom helps in reality. If there is a court battle, as a result of which one parent gains a residence order, it matters little to the other parent that it is no longer described as custody, care and control.

3 To make a split residence order:

This is an order which means that the child resides with one parent for part of the week, month or year, and with the other for the remainder of the week, month or year. Courts may be tempted to make such orders to avoid giving the impression that one parent has won and the other lost. The problem with a split residence order is that it is generally better for a child to know where his or her home is. Dividing the child's time more or less equally between two parents can result in a lack of security and permanence for the child, whatever the satisfaction for the parents.

Other orders the court can make

The court has been given power to make two completely new orders regarding children:

1 Prohibited steps orders

These orders are made when the court wants to limit the parental responsibility of a parent in some specific way.

CASE STUDY

> In an earlier chapter Sarah and Tom, the parents of Luke, were discussed. A residence order has been made in favour of Sarah. Luke attends a school near his home with Sarah. The school does not accept a certain style of haircut and will exclude any boy with that hairstyle.
> Luke is going to have weekend staying contact with Tom, who has told Sarah that he intends to exercise his parental responsibility by having Luke's hair cut in the style banned by the school. Sarah can apply to the court for a prohibited steps order, forbidding Tom to exercise his parental responsibility by having Luke's hair cut in that particular hairstyle.

2 Specific issue orders

These orders are made when there is some specific matter of dispute between parents which they cannot resolve by agreement.

CASE STUDY

> Tom has decided that the school attended by Luke is run by a reactionary and authoritarian head teacher. He wants Luke to change to another local school where hairstyles are a matter of choice. Sarah, on the other hand, is happy with Luke's present school and wishes him to continue there. Either Sarah or Tom can apply to the court to decide on the question of which school Luke should attend. This kind of application results in a specific issue order, when the court settles the matter by coming to its own decision as to which school it will be in Luke's best interests to attend.

Who may apply for orders?

1 Residence, contact, prohibited steps or specific issue orders
(a) Any parent can apply. This includes unmarried fathers.
(b) Any guardian can apply.
(c) Any person with a residence order can apply.

2 Residence or contact orders only
(a) Anyone listed under 1 above.
(b) Anyone married to the parent of a child, who has treated the child as "a child of the family", has the right to apply, even if the marriage has ended.
(c) Anyone with whom a child has lived for a period of at least three years has the right to apply.
(d) Anyone who has the consent of each person with a residence order in respect of the child can apply.
(e) If the child is in the care of a local authority under a care order, anyone with the consent of the local authority can apply.
(f) In any other case, each person with parental responsibility for a child is entitled to apply.

3 Other People
Anyone who is not entitled to make an application under any of the categories set out above may apply to the court for permission to make an application. This includes the child, who will be granted permission if he is considered to be of sufficient understanding and maturity.

Grandparents and other interested relatives or friends of the child can also apply for permission to make an application, if they do not qualify under any of the categories listed above. There will usually be little difficulty in obtaining permission for anyone who can show that it would be in a child's interests for an order to be made.

Effect of residence orders

1   Change of child's surname

If you are considering changing your child's surname do be aware that it is an automatic condition of all residence orders that you have to get the written consent of every person with parental responsibility for the child, or the permission of the court. The court will, in certain circumstances, give permission for a child's surname to be changed, even where one of the child's parents is opposed to the change.

Changing a child's surname is something which should not be done lightly. A court would need to be satisfied that the change is going to be in the interests of the child.

CASE STUDY

> Jemma R's parents divorced and her mother remarried. The new husband was Mr T. Her mother allowed Jemma to be known as Jemma T by friends and neighbours, and registered her at school as "Jemma R known as T". Mr R objected to his daughter being known by the new surname. Jemma's mother applied to the court for leave to change the child's surname.
>
> It was decided that it would not be in Jemma's interests, and would be totally unrealistic, for the court to make an order forbidding the use of the mother's new surname by Jemma. The order would be impossible to enforce. Jemma knew that her real surname was R, but all her friends and schoolteachers called her Jemma T. The court held that it would not be in her interests to have the name by which she was already known changed to her real name.
>
> This case was decided in the early 1980s. Although one can understand the reasoning behind the decision, it should not be taken as an encouragement to mothers to defy the law, which now makes it clear that a child's surname may not be changed without the consent of the other parent or the leave of the court.

A change of surname is a question on which a child might have views of his or her own. In such a case, if the child were to be of sufficient maturity and understanding, the court might grant leave for the child to make an application about a change of surname.

2 Taking a child out of the country

Where a residence order is in force, no person may remove the child from the United Kingdom without either the written consent of every person with parental responsibility or leave of the court.

However, a person who has a residence order may remove the child for a period of less than one month. This is to enable people with residence orders to take children abroad for the purpose of normal holidays.

It sometimes happens that a parent suspects that the parent with the residence order intends to take the child abroad permanently, rather than simply for a holiday. In such a case, the anxious parent can apply for a prohibited steps order, forbidding the parent with the residence order from removing the child.

If the court is satisfied that there is a real risk that the child will not be returned it can make the prohibited steps order.

3 Conditions attached to orders

If the court considers it to be in the interests of a child, it can attach a condition or conditions to a residence order. For example, if the court considered that there was a real risk of a parent with residence taking the child abroad permanently, the court could attach a condition to the residence order to minimise the risk. The condition might be that the parent with residence was not to remove the child from the jurisdiction for any period without leave of the court or the consent of the other parent.

Family assistance orders

Behind all the provisions of the Children Act is the hope that parents will be able to co-operate with one another for the sake of their children. Lawyers and other professionals concerned with families are only too aware of the strength of feeling which exists when relationships have broken down.

Sometimes it is just too much to expect that emotions will cool immediately when disputes have had to be resolved by court proceedings. The win/lose view is likely to persist. The temptation to use the children as weapons in an ongoing conflict between the parents can be irresistible and have disastrous results.

For this reason the courts have been empowered to make family assistance orders. These orders require that a probation officer or local authority social worker should be made available to "advise, assist and (where appropriate) befriend any person named in the order". Social workers have had rather a bad press in recent years and parents sometimes become alarmed at the suggestion that a social worker should be involved with them and their children. But in the case of family assistance orders social workers are there to do just that, assist. Their training enables them to sort out areas of difficulty.

People who may be named in a family assistance order are:

(a) any parent (including an unmarried father);
(b) any guardian;
(c) any person with whom the child is living;
(d) any person in whose favour a contact order is in force;
(e) any child.

Family assistance orders may only be made if the court believes that the circumstances of the case are "exceptional". The court must also be satisfied that the consent of every person (other than the child) named in the order has been obtained to the making of the order.

Family assistance orders are intended to be a temporary assistance in situations where parents or other interested parties find it difficult to communicate directly with one another in the interests of the child with whom they are all concerned. They are made for periods of six months.

It is hoped that, through the skilled intervention of a probation officer or social worker, the adults and/or children involved in situations of emotional difficulty will be helped to put feelings of hurt or bitterness aside in the interests of children.

Does the mother always get the children?

Family lawyers are frequently asked this question when there is a dispute between parents about where children should live. Fathers often believe that they are at a disadvantage when it comes to a court making this kind of decision.

The answer is that parents start off, so far as the law is concerned, on equal terms. There is no particular magic in being a mother. Every child is an individual, with his or her own individual set of characteristics and circumstances. The court will do its utmost to ensure that for the particular child in any case the decision made will be in that child's best interests.

That means taking account of all the circumstances. One circumstance which cannot be ignored is that in most cases it is often thought a baby or a very young child will be more adequately cared for by a mother than a father.

Again, this is not true of all babies or very young children. Many modern fathers are equally capable of caring for their children from babyhood. Some mothers do not provide the best care. Each case will be decided after careful investigation of all the circumstances including, of course, the ascertainable wishes and feelings of the child, if he or she is old enough to understand what is going on.

As children grow older, the undeniable tilt of the scales in the mother's favour becomes less significant. But another factor which will be taken into account, if it exists, is that the mother may be available on a full-time basis to care for the children while the father has a full-time job.

Not every full-time mother succeeds in obtaining a residence order where the father has a full-time job. Again, each case depends on the circumstances.

The guiding principle for the court will always be to discover what will be in the best interests of the child.

Useful Addresses

The National Council for One Parent Families,
255 Kentish Town Road,
London NW5 2LX
Tel: 071 267 1361

The Child Poverty Action Group,
1–5 Bath Street,
London EC1V 9PY
Tel: 071 253 3406

Gingerbread (support for lone parents and their families),
35 Wellington Street,
London WC2E 7BN
Tel: 071 240 0953

Families Need Fathers (helps non-residential parents and their children),
BM Families,
London WC1N 3XX
Tel: 081 886 0970

Children – North East,
la Claremont Street,
Newcastle Upon Tyne NE2 4AH
Tel: 091 232 3741

Parent Network (support and education groups for parents),
44–46 Caversham Road,
London NW5 2DS
Tel: 071 485 8535

Children Need Grandparents (aid and advice to grandparents),
2 Surrey Way,
Laindon West,
Basildon,
Essex SS15 6PS
Tel: 0268 414607

Children's Legal Centre,
20 Compton Terrace,
London N1 2UN
Tel: 071 359 6251

Network of Access and Child Contact Centres (NACCC),
St Andrew's with Castlegate Church,
Goldsmith Street,
Nottingham NG1 5JT
Tel: 0602 484557

Mothers Apart From Their Children (MATCH),
c/o BM Problems,
London WC1N 3XX

Single Parent Links and Special Holidays (SPLASH),
19 North Street,
Plymouth,
Devon PL4 9AH
Tel: 0752 674067

Single Parent Travel Club (SPTC),
37 Sunningdale Park,
Queen Victoria Road,
New Tupton,
Chesterfield S42 6DZ
Tel: 0246 865069

Holidays One-Parents (HOP),
51 Hampshire Road,
Droylsden,
Manchester M43 7PH
Tel: 061 370 0337

7

HOW THE LAW CAN HELP YOU TO REACH AN AGREEMENT

Ideally, when the relationship of parents breaks down, the parents themselves should be able to discuss the future of their children together. Putting their own feelings aside, they should concentrate on the simple truth that, whereas relationships between parents may not necessarily endure, parenthood is for life.

With the increase in the breakdown of relationships, more and more research has been carried out into the effects on the children involved. Not very surprisingly, it is the unanimous view of the experts who have conducted these investigations that the children who best survive the breakdown of the parents' relationship are those whose parents are able to communicate with each other without recrimination and bitterness. Separating or separated parents who can talk to one another about matters concerning their children give the children reassurance that they are still loved and important and will continue to be so.

This is why there has been such an increasing emphasis on trying to help partners to face their problems and seek solutions to them together rather than battling out their differences through the courts. This is known as conciliation.

What Is Conciliation?

The dictionary definition of the verb to conciliate is "to win over from anger or hostility, to win goodwill". Many people confuse conciliation with "reconciliation", and mistakenly believe that a conciliation appointment will mean that attempts will be made to persuade them against separation.

Conciliation is a process of attempting to pour oil on troubled waters. In any dispute a conciliator listens to what each side has to say and then attempts to find some common ground or to negotiate between the disputants to reach an agreement with which both will be reasonably content. There is no attempt, or indeed intent, to arrive at a "kiss and make up" situation.

The Appointment

Conciliation appointments were introduced into the courts as a way of trying to avoid the bitterness and recrimination which frequently arose between warring parents in the course of court proceedings. It has been found to be very helpful to most parents to be given an opportunity to explore the possibilities of agreement on mutual ground with the assistance of a skilled mediator.

It had been the experience of the courts that when evidence of one parent's complaints against the other had been written down, in the form of affidavits or statements for the court, the level of bitterness was bound to escalate. It was therefore decided that a conciliation process at court should be introduced, to take place before any written evidence had been filed or seen by either parent.

The advantages of the conciliation appointment are

(a) it gives the parents a chance to reach agreement, with the assistance of skilled help and before written allegations made by one against the other exacerbate an already difficult situation;
(b) if successful, it results in great savings in time and expense.

Will there always be a conciliation appointment?

It is usual for the court to fix a conciliation appointment where there is a dispute about a child between the child's parents. However, a conciliation appointment is not always fixed in applications about children. If the court considers that the level of bitterness between the parents is such that there is no realistic possibility of conciliation being successful, it may not fix the appointment.

What happens at the appointment?

Once the application about the child has been filed with the court, whether by a solicitor acting for a parent or by a parent himself or herself, the date and time fixed for the conciliation appointment will be given to both parents. The appointment will be with a District Judge of the court where the application has been made. The District Judge will take the appointment, together with a court welfare officer.

Who should attend the appointment?

Each of the parents should attend the appointment, together with legal advisers if any. The children should also be brought to the appointment, if they are over nine years of age, and sometimes even younger children attend.

Do not be worried by this appointment as usually the atmosphere is as relaxed and informal as possible. When the case is called on, the parents and their legal advisers, if they are legally represented, will go into the court. Normally, in the court of a district judge, everyone sits around a long table. The district judge will be at the top of the table, with the court welfare officer. The parents and legal advisers sit on either side of the table.

The district judge will introduce the welfare officer to the parents. If the parent making the application is legally represented, the barrister or solicitor representing him or her will briefly tell the district judge about the application. The judge will be informed about the dates of birth of the children concerned, when and in what circumstances the parents separated, and about the application itself. The facts should be stated neutrally, since the whole aim of the appointment is, as far as humanly possible, to avoid an atmosphere where one parent scores points against the other. The barrister or solicitor representing the other parent will then be given an opportunity to define the area of disagreement, and should again be taking care to be as non-controversial as possible.

If one or both parents are in person, unrepresented by a barrister or solicitor, the district judge may ask a few direct questions in order to clarify the areas of dispute.

Any children who are attending the conciliation appointment will be asked to wait outside the court while these preliminary introductions are going on.

The conciliation process

Everyone then comes out of the court, hopefully into some reasonably comfortable area. In the Principal Registry of the Family Division, in London, conciliation appointments take place in a suite of rooms which have been furnished with comfortable chairs and equipped with a machine which dispenses hot and cold drinks, crisps, biscuits and confectionery. This helps to promote a relaxed and friendly atmosphere, which is vitally important to the whole idea of conciliation.

Unfortunately, conditions in other courts around the country vary enormously, with the worst – all too frequent – situation being that the parents, the children and their legal advisers all sit on hard benches ranged along the walls of some dreary court corridor, where there are no refreshment facilities and an atmosphere calculated to make everyone concerned feel thoroughly miserable. Not really conducive to the conciliation process!

The court welfare officer decides how to handle the conciliation process. This will almost certainly involve, in no particular order, discussing the dispute

(a) with the parents together without the children;
(b) with each of the parents on their own;
(c) with the children, sometimes together and sometimes singly, depending on the circumstances of the case;
(d) with the parents and children all together.

The whole process can be very short or it might take as long as a day. The idea is for the welfare officer first to identify the precise areas of dispute between the parents. He or she then attempts to find any areas where there may be agreement. From that point, attempts will be made to negotiate a full agreement on the points disputed, helping the parents to bear in mind that it is unlikely that one or the other will achieve exactly what he or she wants, and that it is infinitely better to settle matters between themselves than to have a solution imposed by the court, which may not be acceptable to either of them.

The attendance of the children, if they are old enough, is of vital importance. It often happens that a child is too torn between loyalties to be able to tell one or both parents what his or her view of the dispute might be. The welfare officer will be skilled in relating to children and will frequently be able to communicate the child's wishes and feelings about the dispute to both parents, sometimes with the result that any disagreements can be resolved there and then.

What is the point of having lawyers there?

If one or both parents is legally represented a barrister or solicitor will attend the conciliation appointment with that parent. Unusually for court appointments, the lawyer will be – or ought to be – keeping a low profile. However, if a settlement of the dispute is being negotiated, the parents might wish to consult their legal advisers, who will be able to assist with the drafting of a consent order to be made by the court should any agreement be reached.

If the conciliation appointment has been successful and the parents have reached agreement, everyone goes back into the court before the judge, who makes the order which has been agreed. In some cases, agreement is such that the judge might decide that it is preferable to make no order at all, since the parents, after discussion with the welfare officer, have decided to exercise their own parental responsibility for making decisions about their children without the necessity for a court order.

On the other hand, if the conciliation has not been successful, everyone goes back into court and the judge gives directions for how the case will continue.

Where no agreement has been reached the Judge will almost certainly order the preparation of a court welfare officer's report, directed to the question in dispute. However, the welfare officer who makes the report will not be the one who has been involved in the conciliation appointment. This is to ensure that nothing said by anyone in the course of a conciliation appointment can affect the evidence given to the court when the case comes to be heard.

Confidentiality

Do be assured that nothing which is said by anyone in the course of a conciliation appointment can be repeated in any subsequent hearing of the matter by the court, whether in writing in a statement filed with the court or in oral evidence. The legal expression for this is that the discussions which take place during conciliation are "privileged".

CASE STUDY

Jeremy has applied for contact with his daughter Angela, who is six years old. Angela's mother, Joan, is opposed to Jeremy having any contact with her. Jeremy and Joan separated when Angela was two years old and Angela has not seen her father since then. Joan says that Angela has forgotten her father. Joan has a new husband, Peter, who has taken over the role of father in Angela's life.

A conciliation appointment is arranged. Jeremy and Joan attend the appointment. In the course of discussions with the court welfare officer, Joan admits in Jeremy's presence that the principal reason for her opposition to the reintroduction of Jeremy into Angela's life is Peter's jealousy of Jeremy.

The conciliation appointment is not successful. Jeremy's application for contact will have to be heard by a Judge and the judge gives directions for signed statements to be filed by Jeremy and Joan, setting out their respective positions. It appears to Jeremy that the fact that Peter is unreasonably jealous of him is not a good reason for denying him contact with Angela.

In his signed statement or in his oral evidence to the court when his application is heard, can Jeremy refer to Joan's admission that her principal reason for refusing to agree to his having contact with Angela is that Peter is jealous of Jeremy?

The answer must be no. What Joan told the court welfare officer in Jeremy's presence during the conciliation process is privileged. Jeremy may not refer to it in his statement or in his oral evidence.

The exception to the rule of confidentiality

There is one exception to the privilege which is given to anything which is said in the course of a conciliation appointment. The exception is when anything is said which indicates that a child might be at serious risk.

For example, suppose during the conciliation discussions Joan had admitted to the court welfare officer that, on occasions when she had lost her temper with Angela, she had been slapping her much too hard, to the extent that she had twice bruised the little girl so badly that she had kept her away from school so that the bruising would not be noticed. The privilege attached to the conciliation process would be overridden by the primary duty to have regard to the best interests of Angela, and her mother's disclosure could be reported by the court welfare officer to the social services department for the area where Joan and Angela were living.

There have been attempts to persuade the court that discussions which took place in the course of conciliation or mediation were not strictly privileged, so that things said by one or other person or by the conciliator might be disclosed if they were at all relevant to the case.

However, the Court of Appeal made the position clear in a recent case, when it was stated that evidence could not be given of statements made by people in the course of conciliation sessions "save in the very unusual case where a statement is made clearly indicating that the maker has in the past caused or is likely in the future to cause serious harm to the wellbeing of a child".

The reasons for Confidentiality

This confidentiality demonstrates the importance which the courts attach to encouraging people who are caught up in family disputes to try to resolve them with skilled help rather than taking them to a full-scale court battle.

People will be less worried about possible repercussions if they can be assured that what they say in the process of mediation or conciliation will remain completely confidential. With the reduction in eligibility for legal aid, the mediation process is likely to seem an infinitely more attractive – because much less expensive – way of resolving conflicts than slugging them out in court.

This can only be to the ultimate advantage of parents – and more importantly to the advantage of the unfortunate children at the centre of parental quarrels.

8

THE COURT WELFARE
REPORT

If you are involved in a case concerning your child, the court may
ask for a welfare report. This is nothing to be concerned about; it
is simply used to assist the court to reach a decision. The court will
direct that the report should deal with a specific question or questions,
and any report prepared will normally be limited to those questions.
However, it occasionally happens that a report will deal with wider
matters concering the child and the various people involved, rather
than limiting itself strictly to the areas indicated by the court.

The purpose of welfare reports is to assist the court by giving a
fuller picture of the child's situation and all the factors relevant to
any decision the court is being asked to make. For example, if there
is a dispute about with which parent a child should live the welfare
officer will visit the child in both homes, or if there is a dispute about
contact the welfare officer may decide to observe the child's reaction
to the parent who wants contact. By ordering a welfare report the
court is *not* handing over the task of making the decision to a welfare
officer. The decision is for the court alone.

However, it is true to say that the court will almost always pay a
great deal of attention to any recommendation made in a welfare
report. Indeed, if a judge does not make an order in accordance
with a recommendation by a court welfare officer, he must state his
reasons for not doing so.

Not every welfare report contains recommendations about the
decisions which the court is being asked to make. Some welfare
reports simply set out the information which the officer has been

able to obtain, possibly together with some impressions of the various people interviewed in the course of the investigations, but make no firm recommendation on what should be the order made, leaving it to the court to make the final decision.

The Form of the Report

Welfare reports may be made in writing or orally. If the matter is not one of urgency, it is usual for the court to request a written report. One of the reasons for this is in order to give the parties involved in the court proceedings some notice of what the welfare officer will be saying or recommending. This means that consideration can be given to questions which might be asked of the officer who prepared the report.

Oral reports by court welfare officers

However, if the matter is very urgent, or if for some other reason the court considers it preferable, the report may be requested on the basis that the reporting officer will give only an oral report.

CASE STUDY

Matthew, who is ten years old, is living with his mother Anne and her new husband James, as a result of the court deciding that Matthew should live with his mother. Sam, Matthew's father, has been allowed to have Matthew staying with him for alternate weekends.

Sam goes to court one Monday morning. He asks the judge to discharge the existing residence order in Anne's favour and to make an order that Matthew should live with him. He says that when the child had been due to return to his mother on the previous evening he had broken down in tears and had begged Sam to let him stay with him. Sam says that Matthew was so distressed that he was unable to persuade him to go back. Matthew had told him that he hated James, and that James was punishing him excessively and unfairly, by locking him in a dark cupboard for hours on end.

The judge is faced with an extremely difficult situation. Sam has informed Anne of his application and she too has come to court to ask for an order that Matthew should be returned to her immediately. She categorically denies that James has been punishing Matthew by locking him in an unlit cupboard. She says that Sam is probably making all this up because he wants Matthew to live with him.

It is in this kind of case that a judge might well ask a welfare officer to talk to Matthew and report back on an oral basis, rather than waiting for a written report, which might very well take weeks or months to prepare. It is obviously an urgent matter. Judges are reluctant to change existing orders without good reason. They are even more reluctant to do so on an emergency basis, preferring to wait until all possible evidence, including a welfare report if appropriate, is before the court.

On the other hand, if Sam is accurately reporting what has been said by Matthew, there is clearly cause for concern about whether he should return to his mother.

In such an urgent situation, where a judge has asked a welfare officer for an oral report, the period of time given for the preparation of the report might be a few days, or even a few hours. It is even possible for a court welfare officer to be requested to see both parents and the child in the court building so as to be able to report back immediately.

The welfare officer would undoubtedly speak to Sam and Anne before attempting to talk to Matthew. He or she would then expect to be introduced to Matthew, by the parents if possible.

Fortunately, the vast majority of court welfare officers are highly skilled and very tactful people. For example, it is extremely unlikely that the welfare officer would ask Matthew straight away whether he has any problems with his stepfather. He or she would have to approach the matter as seems best at the time. It would be usual for the officer to sit down somewhere quietly with the child, hopefully in a room comfortably furnished for such meetings, and simply have a general chat with him.

Matthew might be asked about his school, what subjects he likes best, which games he prefers. The welfare officer might then ask him about his friends, both school friends and those he plays with when he is at home. Gradually, and in a natural way, the welfare officer would take time to encourage Matthew to feel relaxed. Only when Matthew's confidence had been gained would the welfare officer approach the question of what was troubling Matthew, possibly by way of an enquiry about with which parent he was living and how often he saw the other parent.

In this way, the discussion could eventually get to a point where the welfare officer could discuss Matthew's reluctance to return home. It is possible that Matthew has indeed good cause to complain about his stepfather's treatment of him. On the other hand, it is not unknown for a parent with whom the child does not live to "manufacture" complaints, for example by encouraging a child to give a wildly exaggerated account of perfectly normal discipline.

When the officer feels ready to make a report in a case like Matthew's, the parents return to the court and the welfare officer reports the discussion with Matthew to the judge. The judge will

then give each of the parents, or their legal representatives, an
opportunity to put questions to the officer and to make any
submissions as to what the decision about Matthew should be.
The judge then makes a decision based upon all the evidence which
he has read and heard.

Written reports

Matthew's case was one of emergency. Most reports made by court
welfare officers are prepared in writing and at a much more leisurely
pace. Conciliation appointments have already been discussed in
Chapter 7. However, there are cases where disputes between parents
can only be resolved by a court hearing. In these cases a court welfare
officer will be asked to investigate the dispute and provide a full
written report. A different welfare officer will be appointed so that
anything said during conciliation remains confidential.

How long will it take?

One of the stated aims of the Children Act was the avoidance of delay
in deciding questions relating to children. Judges hearing children's
cases are always very keen to have them decided as quickly as
possible, to avoid causing unnecessary stress to parents, and more
importantly to children.

In an ideal world this would mean that delays were kept to
a minimum in children cases. Unfortunately, although everyone
concerned is committed to moving things along as quickly as possible,
financial constraints mean that families frequently have to wait for
periods of several months before a case can be heard.

The time taken to prepare welfare reports varies from court to
court; a period of three to four months is not at all unusual. Some
courts will fix a hearing date before the welfare report has been made
available, other courts will not fix a date until the report has actually
been filed.

If the court waits until the welfare report has actually been filed,
there may well be a further delay of several months before a hearing
date can be given. This means that it is not at all uncommon for cases
to take six months, and sometimes even up to and more than a year,
to come before the court.

When one looks at this in human terms it can result in enormous
frustration and even downright misery for the parents and children
concerned.

CASE STUDY

David and Cheryl have become unhappy in their marriage and have decided to divorce. They have four children, Donna who is thirteen years old, Alan who is ten years old, Susannah who is six years old and Charlie who is five years old. David and Cheryl have been quite unable to agree with whom the children should live after they separate. Each has applied to the court asking for the children to live with him or her.

There has been a conciliation appointment, attended by the children as well as by David and Cheryl. The court welfare officer was unable to help the parents to reach agreement. A welfare report, which will be prepared by a different officer, has been ordered.

David and Cheryl occupy a semi-detached house which they are buying with a mortgage in their joint names. It is accepted that whoever has the children will continue to live in the home. The other parent will leave.

Neither David nor Cheryl is prepared to leave until the court decides which of them is to have the children. The house has only three bedrooms, the third of which is very small. Since David moved out of their bedroom, Cheryl has been sharing the main bedroom with Susannah. Alan and Charlie share the second bedroom and Donna has the very small bedroom. David has a put-u-up bed in the living-room.

David and Cheryl try to behave in a normal way for the sake of the children. But the tensions are quite obvious and have their effects upon the children. Cheryl does not cook meals for David and she does no washing or ironing for him. She and David barely speak to one another. The whole atmosphere in the home is highly stressful. Donna's school work is suffering, Alan has become cheeky and is getting out of control, Susannah is weepy and clingy, and Charlie has started bed-wetting, having been dry at night since he was two.

The situation of David and Cheryl and their children is a distressingly common one. Neither parent will agree to leave the home until the matter has been decided by the court, for fear that the other parent would gain the advantage of the "status quo" argument.

"Status quo" is an expression which is popular with lawyers involved in family cases, particularly where there are disputes about residence. Roughly translated, it means "the situation as it exists". Lawyers arguing a case will place great emphasis on the benefits to a child of not interfering with the status quo – the situation to which the child is accustomed.

It cannot be denied that court welfare officers and judges are reluctant to interfere with the status quo, where it appears to be working reasonably well, in case such interference would bring about a worse situation. It follows that if you are the parent who is actually caring for a child when a dispute about residence comes to court, you have an undoubted advantage.

It is for this reason that a family lawyer would be unable to advise

either David or Cheryl to leave the home pending a resolution of the
dispute about who is to be the day-to-day carer for the children.
The parent who left would immediately be giving the other the
advantage.

Unfortunately far too many families are forced to live in a
stressful situation such as that experienced by David and Cheryl.
Unless more resources can be directed towards the provision of
an increased number of court welfare officers, court buildings and
judges there seems little hope that such families can be spared
prolonged unhappiness.

The Preparation of the Report

Once a written report has been ordered by the court, the welfare
officer has the duty to investigate all those matters to which the
court directs the officer's attention. The reporting officer might be
requested to examine the more general question of time spent with
each parent or something more specific such as a choice of school for
a child.

Welfare reports can be ordered in any case concerning a child. If
a grandparent or other interested adult should make an application
with regard to a child, a report can be ordered by the court just as
in disputes between parents.

The welfare officer will read any documentation available on the
court file. Sometimes there will be statements by the parents, and
other witnesses, if these have been ordered by the court. In other
cases the court might direct that no statements should be filed until
all parties have had a chance to read the report. Often a statement will
contain things which will anger one party. For this reason the court
will often delay asking for statements, in order to keep the heat out
of the situation for as long as possible while attempts are being made
to bring the parties to agreement by means of conciliation.

Court welfare officers are, of course, individuals. Each one
approaches the task of preparing a report in his or her individual
way, but there are certain guidelines which the courts have given
them to follow.

CASE STUDY

Delia and Kevin have a six-year-old son, Colin. Delia and Kevin are
living apart. Each has applied to the court for Colin to live with
them. There was a conciliation appointment but it did not result in

an agreement about where Colin should live. The court has ordered a welfare report, to be directed to the question of whether it will be in Colin's best interests to live with his mother or his father.

Delia lives in the home she originally shared with Kevin, a two-bedroom flat. No one else lives there. Kevin has moved to another two-bedroom flat, so the accommodation which could be offered to the child by each parent is roughly the same.

The court welfare officer interviews Delia, alone and with Colin. Both interviews take place in Delia's flat. The court welfare officer interviews Kevin, alone and with Colin. Both these interviews take place at the offices of social services for the area.

The court welfare officer then files his report. The report ends with a firm recommendation that Delia's application should be granted and Kevin's rejected.

There may well be many good reasons for the recommendation made by the court welfare officer that Colin should live with his mother rather than with his father. But Kevin would have a legitimate reason to challenge the report and its recommendation. Because the Court of Appeal have made it clear that, when a report is ordered relating to the question of with which parent a child is to live, the child should be observed by the court welfare officer with each of the parents in his or her home environment.

A welfare officer who does not carry out that duty to see the child in both homes runs the risk that any recommendations given will be viewed as of little help in the decision-making process for the judge.

Indeed, in a residence dispute where a welfare officer has not taken the trouble to visit the child in both homes, the court might well order a further report to be made by the officer after visits to each home have been carried out.

The child's wishes and feelings

One of the most important considerations for the court in any question relating to a child is the wishes and feelings of that child. As has already been pointed out, the older the child, the more he or she can understand and appreciate what the dispute is about, the more regard the court will pay to what he/she wants.

In most cases about children which have to be decided by the court, the person who will explore the child's wishes and feelings and communicate them to the court will be the welfare officer.

It has to be remembered that when arguments about children get as far as a court hearing, adult emotions and even tempers are likely to be running at a high level. For example, it would be most unusual for any parent to continue a battle about where children should live without being absolutely convinced in his or her own mind that the children's wishes and feelings were identical with his or hers.

The temptation for a parent involved in such a dispute to encourage the child to tell the court welfare officer what the parent wants the officer to hear can be too great in some cases. This leads to the desperately sad situation where a child can be subjected to the most unbearable emotional pressure by one or both parents. The parent becomes so wrapped up in determination to "win" that the effects of the emotional temperature on the child are completely disregarded.

There are cases where parents simply never give up on the battle, even after a court decision has been made. Some parents will go on subjecting their children to pressure, just to get back at the other parent. The unfortunate children of such parents often bear the emotional scars into their adult lives.

Questioning the court welfare officer

The report of the court welfare officer will normally be filed some time before the hearing date, and copies will be sent to all concerned. At this stage, as at all stages, the parents can and often do make their own decision without the need for a court hearing. But if there has to be a hearing the judge will give each of the parties or their legal representatives, if any, an opportunity to question the court welfare officer. If you are representing yourself and you wish to ask a welfare officer questions about the report, you must ask the court to ensure that the officer will be available on the day of the hearing.

If you yourself are asking the questions, it is a good idea to make a list of them before coming to court. Always ask the questions as politely as you can. The judge will never be impressed by rudeness to the court welfare officer, and you can be quite sure that the judge will listen with close attention to any questions you may ask, and to the replies given, before coming to a decision.

After the hearing

Some court welfare officers will offer to make themselves available to the parties to give advice and assistance on an informal basis after the hearing. This can often be very helpful in smoothing initial difficulties.

9

CHILD SUPPORT

Until April 1993, when the parents of a child had separated, the usual means of obtaining a financial contribution towards the maintenance of the child was by way of a court order. There were cases, of course, where the parents were able to agree what the contribution should be and then there would be no need for an order of the court.

You will probably have seen many news reports about absent fathers being chased for maintenance. This has come about due to the Child Support Act which came into force in 1993 and completely changed the approach to child maintenance. It is perhaps rather too early to predict how the Act will work out in practice, but there is no doubt that its operation is stirring up considerable controversy.

Background

The objectives behind the child support legislation were understandable. First, it formed part of an overall determination by the government to emphasise that parents were responsible for their own children. In 1989, the Children Act had started the process of underlining the fact that being a parent carries responsibilities rather than rights. In 1991, the Criminal Justice Act had extended the powers of the court to impose penalties on those with parental responsibility for delinquent children. The Child Support Act was the third plank in the government's programme.

Financial considerations were of considerable significance. There had been growing concern about the level of payments being ordered by courts and the resultant burden on the state when social security payments had to make up the difference between the maintenance ordered and income support rates.

Throughout the 1980s there had been attempts made to persuade courts to make orders in line with current income support rates, but these had largely been unsuccessful. In 1990, the average maintenance being ordered for a child, of any age up to eighteen, was £18 per week. In that year, the National Foster Care Association was recommending payments of £34.02 per week for a child under the age of five.

Increasing numbers of parents were separating, and the consequently increased burden upon the taxpayer was becoming insupportable. Having failed to get the courts to raise the level of orders being made, the government decided to set up the Child Support Agency as a completely separate entity, which would be under governmental control.

Unfortunately, it soon became clear that there are aspects of the child support scheme which are causing considerable public disquiet. Hopefully, most of these are simply teething problems which can be remedied by fine tuning.

"Caring" and "absent"?

Probably one of the most tactless aspects of the child support scheme is in its use of terminology. It ought to have been foreseeable that to describe parents as either "caring" or "absent" was going to cause trouble. This should have been particularly obvious in the context of the Children Act which had just deliberately enacted the words "residence" and "contact" in place of the emotive "custody" and "access".

Not every parent who does not have day-to-day care of his or her child is in that position from choice. Moreover, many parents who do not care for their children on a day-to-day basis are still concerned, loving parents who wish to play as full a part in the lives of the children as possible.

Not surprisingly, such parents find being categorised as "absent" hurtful, particularly when it is contrasted with "caring". It should have been possible to exchange those words for something neutral like "residential" and "non-residential". Perhaps it is not too late for something to be done.

The Formula

The financial contribution which must be made by the absent parent for the maintenance of his or her child is now calculated by means of a formula. The formula is fairly rigid and is not particularly easy to understand.

On the plus side, the rigidity of the formula means that every absent parent has his or her contribution worked out in accordance with a strict mathematical calculation which is applied in every case. This is to be contrasted with the somewhat haphazard situation in operation before the Child Support legislation, which meant that two judges sitting in the same court in different cases might make two completely different maintenance orders given the same figures to work on.

There have been criticisms that the formula does not make allowance for some of the outgoings of the absent parent, to the point where he or she can be reduced to an income below that of income support by its operation. Payment of instalments in relation to certain debts is not taken into account, for example.

If the absent parent lives at some distance from the children, cost of travel to and from contact visits is not taken into account. This is another matter which has caused considerable concern.

Second wives bitterly resent the levels of contribution being sought by the Child Support Agency for the children of their husbands' first marriages, particularly where the first wife has remarried and lives in comfortable financial circumstances with her new husband.

Pre-existing Agreements or Orders

Loud complaints have been voiced by fathers who believe that they are being asked to contribute twice over because of agreements or orders made before the Child Support legislation came into force.

CASE STUDY

Bruce and Maggie divorced in 1987, when their children were aged two, three and five. Bruce agreed that Maggie should have their jointly owned matrimonial home transferred into her sole name, in full and final settlement of any financial claims which Maggie might have against him for herself, and on the understanding that Maggie would not seek to obtain any order for maintenance for the children.

It was explained to Bruce and Maggie by their legal advisers that Maggie's claims for herself could be dismissed, in accordance with their agreement. However, the court had no power to dismiss the claims of the children. The court would make a nominal order for each of the children, at the rate of 5p per year. Bruce believed that that was the end of the matter.

Maggie had agreed not to pursue a claim for the children. Before the Child Support legislation it would have been extremely difficult for Maggie to persuade a court to ask for maintenance for the children. Bruce would have produced documentary evidence of the agreement, correspondence between solicitors perhaps.

But today, Maggie and the children are living on income support. The Child Support Agency does not take into account the agreement made between Maggie and Bruce, even though Bruce gave up his share in the matrimonial home in exchange for Maggie's promise that she would not seek maintenance for the children. The children are still young, so Bruce faces several more years of liability for maintenance payments which he believed would never be sought.

There are many absent fathers who are in the same position as Bruce. The courts had, for many years, been in favour of what were called "clean break" orders. These were orders like the consent order made in Bruce and Maggie's case, which seemed to finalise financial matters between the parties to a divorce, leaving the husband and the wife free to make new lives for themselves.

Suddenly, Bruce's clean break no longer exists. Understandably, he feels outraged. He would never have agreed to give up his interest in the matrimonial home, which amounted to several thousands of pounds, had he realised that Maggie's promise could not be kept.

When the Child Support law was passed there was a good deal of debate among lawyers about whether, in the circumstances of a case like Bruce's, a father might be able to bring a successful late appeal against the order to which he had consented. But the courts have never made orders which completely extinguished a child's right to maintenance, because it has never been considered that a mother ought to have the power to agree that the child should have no right to financial support from his or her father. Invariably, a "clean break" order where there was still a relevant child would have included a nominal order for maintenance by the father, probably of 5p a year. This was to emphasise that the child's right had not been extinguished and that if there were to be a really important change in circumstances – for example if the mother had been seriously injured in a road traffic accident – the father could still be expected to contribute. So it has now been decided that a father like Bruce has no right to re-open a case where there has been a clean break agreement, since he ought to have realised that the child still had a right to maintenance, even if the mother had agreed not to pursue that right. It is obviously hard on a father, who believed that there was an agreement between himself and the mother, to find that the state can and will ignore that agreement, and there is no doubt that the introduction of the Child Support legislation has caused a good deal of bitterness among fathers like Bruce.

Natural Fathers

The parents liable to maintain a child under the Child Support legislation are the child's natural parents. Before the Child Support Act came into force, a father would have been liable for any child he had treated as a child of the family during the marriage. This change in the law is likely to have two consequences.

CASE STUDY

> When Ben met Sherrie she had a baby, Rachel, who was a few months old. Ben and Sherrie married and Ben always treated Rachel as his own child. Ben and Sherrie later had two more children, Marcel and Barnabas. If Ben and Sherrie separated Ben would be liable to maintain Marcel and Barnabas under child support law, but not Rachel, even though he always treated Rachel in exactly the same way as his own children. This would probably leave Rachel, now a teenager, feeling hurt and bewildered that there should be a difference between her and her brothers, when she has always looked on Ben as her own father too.
>
> Sherrie is on income support. The child support officer asks her to name Rachel's father so that he can be traced and made to pay maintenance for Rachel.

Naming the father

It is a requirement of the Child Support legislation that a mother on income support should identify the natural father of her child. If she refuses to do so, she can be penalised by a reduction in the amount of benefit she is paid, unless she can demonstrate that to identify the father would put her or any child living with her at risk.

This provision has the unfortunate practical result that a father who has used violence against the mother or a child in the past will be able to evade responsibility for Child Support. In the circumstances, it is hardly surprising if responsible and law-abiding fathers believe that the operation of the Child Support legislation is producing an unfair result.

As only the natural father of a child is liable for maintenance under the operation of the Child Support law, it is predicted that some fathers will seek to deny paternity in order to escape liability. Under the old law, if a child had been accepted as a child of the family by the father, he would be liable to maintain that child when his marriage broke down. It is more than possible that many fathers who suspected that a child was not theirs during a marriage may now wish to put that suspicion to the test.

Unfortunately, applications made in such circumstances may well have serious repercussions so far as the unfortunate child is concerned, not to mention the effect upon the relationship between the divorced parents.

Changing the child's residence

There is a possibility that many absent parents will seek to vary custody or residence orders rather than take on the heavy burden of payments under the new method of assessment. How sympathetic the reaction of courts will be to applications made by absent parents in those circumstances remains to be seen.

On such an application, the court must consider all the relevant circumstances. The possibility that the absent parent's new relationship, of which there may be further children, may be endangered by an order to make substantial payments to the first family could be something which the court might take into account. The interests of all children concerned will obviously be paramount. In a case where the child's interests would be as well met with one parent as with the other – and there are many such – it might well be that on balance a judge would take the view that the original order should be varied to relieve a father of an insupportable financial burden. This would be a likely outcome where a father would have found it impossible to travel to have contact with a child had he had to make the payments assessed, and where the court took the view that the child's interests would be equally well served were he to live with his father as his mother.

Parents with care will no doubt be resentful of applications to vary the arrangements for children which are precipitated by financial motives. Again, these situations will not help to keep relations between separated parents on an amicable basis. A deterioration in the relationship between their parents is never in the best interests of children.

The Future

These are just a few of the problems which the new Child Support legislation is likely to bring to light. At the time of writing it has only been in operation for a year and its effectiveness remains to be seen. It has already given rise to vehement opposition and several groups have been formed to organise public demonstrations of protest against it. It seems likely that some modifications will have to be introduced.

However, it is difficult to see what could have been done to ensure that children were properly maintained by their parents in the absence of such legislation. Family breakdown is so common now that it is simply unrealistic to expect the taxpayer to underwrite the support of the parent with care for ever. The enormous changes in the structure of the family meant that there had to be a new approach to the mechanism of Child Support.

The problems must be overcome and the formula adapted, if necessary. But, whatever the protesters say, it would appear that there is no alternative to the concept of child support, especially for lone single mothers on income support. If you are a parent concerned about Child Support and want to know more about Child Support legislation contact your Citizens Advice Bureau or local county court where you will be given a free leaflet which gives full details.

Applying for Child Support Maintenance

When you must apply

If you are a parent who has care of your child and you are in receipt of income support or disability working allowance, of if your partner

is someone who gets one of those benefits, you have to apply for an
assessment of Child Support maintenance if you are asked to do so
by the Child Support Agency. However, if you believe that giving
information about the absent parent would lead to harm or undue
distress for you or any child living with you, the Agency may agree
that you do not have to give the information.

Who else can apply?

Anyone who is a parent and has the child or children living with her
or him when the other parent lives elsewhere can apply to the Child
Support Agency, as long as both parents live in Great Britain or
Northern Ireland. You can also apply if you are caring for a child of
whom you are not the parent. A telephone enquiry number which
you can call is given at the end of this chapter. Absent parents can
also apply for a Child Support assessment to be made.

What happens if a child spends time with both parents?

It your child spends part of the time with you and part of the time
with the other parent, the Child Support maintenance will be shared,
provided that the child spends an average of two nights a week, at
least 104 nights a year, with the absent parent.

How will the agency contact absent parents?

If you are the parent with care you will be asked to give information
about the absent parent, for example his name and address and date
of birth. If you do not know the address the Agency will try to find
it by, for example, checking national insurance and inland revenue
records. The Agency will not give the address of one parent to the
other without the agreement of both parents.

What happens if the absent parent refuses to give information?

If the absent parent refuses to complete the form which is sent
requesting details of his or her income and outgoings the Agency
can make an interim assessment, which will usually be higher than

the assessment which would be made with full information about the absent parent's means. The absent parent will then be compelled to pay at the interim assessment rate until he or she provides sufficient information for a full assessment to be made.

How does an absent parent pay?

If you are an absent parent you can pay directly to the parent with care by cheque, standing order or postal order. Alternatively, you can make the payments through the Child Support Agency by direct debit, post office transcash or through a bank to the agency's account. The payments can be made weekly, monthly, or at some other agreed intervals. If the absent parent does not make the payments assessed, and does not have an acceptable reason for failing to do so, the Agency can have the payments deducted from the parent's wages or salary at source. However, if an absent parent's financial circumstances change he or she can apply for a new assessment to be made. If you are an absent parent who is on income support and you are over eighteen, fit for work and with no dependent children living with you, you may be required to contribute £2.20 per week towards the maintenance of your children.

How much will it cost?

Annual reviews are carried out. The standard annual fee which is charged by the Child Support Agency for its assessment and review service is £44, which has to be paid by each parent, unless you are in one of the following groups:

(a) you or your live-in partner gets income support, family credit or disability working allowance;
(b) you are under sixteen, or under nineteen and in full-time education up to A-level or equivalent;
(c) your income falls below certain limits.

Collection service

The Child Support Agency offers a collection service in addition to the assessment and review service. If asked to do so it will collect the payments from the absent parent and pass them on to the parent with care. If the absent parent falls behind with the payments the

Agency will consider taking action to enforce them. The standard annual fee for the collection service is £34, and both parents will be expected to pay this when either of them asks the agency for the collection service. However, the absent parent has to pay this fee if the parent with care is getting income support, family credit or disability working allowance.

Useful Information

Child Support Agency Enquiry Line:
Tel: 0345 133 133 (9 a.m.–6 p.m. weekdays; calls charged at local rate)

Child Support Agency,
PO Box 55,
Brierley Hill,
West Midlands DY5 1YL

For Parents Who Live Apart – leaflet issued by DSS explaining Child Support (NI 19) obtainable in post offices, local benefit offices, county court offices, Citizens Advice Bureaux, etc.

III

Someone Else's Child

10

ADOPTION

Adoption usually brings to mind a picture of a lovely newborn baby being handed into the care of an adoring young couple, who have been yearning for a child of their own and will care for the child until he or she grows into adulthood, just as though they had been the birth parents. Adopting a child can sometimes be like that, but not in the majority of cases. Unfortunately, the reality is that of the 30,000+ children currently waiting for adoptive parents nearly half are over the age of nine. Of these some will be hoping for adopters who will take on brothers or sisters as well, sometimes up to four at a time!

To adopt a child is to take that child into your family. It should be just as important to you and to the child as giving birth to your own child. Once the adoption order has been made by the court, the child becomes part of the family into which he or she has been adopted. Links with birth parents, natural brothers and sisters, grandparents and other members of the extended birth family are usually, but not always, completely severed. The new parents of an adopted child take on all the legal and moral responsibilities towards that child that they would have had if he or she had been their natural child.

Obviously, since adoption is such an exciting and important step for a child and for the adopters, great care has to be taken and a full investigation made before an adoption order can be contemplated. Adoption orders can only be made by the courts, and then after the most detailed enquiry has been made into whether it is in the best interests of the child.

You might be surprised to learn that it was not possible for anyone to adopt a child legally in this country until the Adoption Act was passed in 1976.

In 1977, the year after the Act was passed, nearly 13,000 children were adopted. But there has been a decline in the annual number of adoptions since then. In 1993 approximately 7,000 children were adopted, and in approximately half of those cases the adoption was by a step-parent or by some member of the child's birth family.

This is important when you realise that children who have been adopted by step-parents or members of their birth families are not children who were available generally for adoption, meaning the number of actual adoptions is much lower than one might first think.

Sadly, this drop in the real number does not mean that there are fewer couples who would like to adopt, nor does it mean that there are no children available for adoption. The reasons are far more complicated. First, the increased availability of contraception has meant there are less unwanted children born. Another factor has been the change in society's approach to unmarried motherhood. Within living memory, to be an unmarried mother was to experience shame and ostracism which even extended to the unfortunate child. Today, an unmarried mother may keep her baby if she so wishes, without any fear of society's disapproval.

Adoption agencies have no problem in finding adoptive parents for babies and very young children who become available entirely or mainly because their natural families are unable or unwilling to keep them. The demand for such babies far exceeds the supply.

Older children are more difficult to match with prospective adopters. It is understandable that a couple should wish to be the "first" parents of a child they adopt. When a child is old enough to have memories of his birth family, or even a foster family, it is not nearly so easy to match the child with adoptive parents, particularly if the birth family wish to have some ongoing contact after the adoption. Still more difficult to place are the children who have experienced significant abuse of one kind or another during their early years, and who may have continuing psychological problems which cause them to be disturbed in their behaviour and difficult to handle.

Where Do You Begin?

If you want to adopt a child, you must first contact an adoption agency. A list is supplied at the end of this chapter. Adoption is such an important and irrevocable step in the life of a child that an adoption order can only be made by a civil court. Local authority social services departments and voluntary adoption agencies all have adoption panels. Members of these panels include experienced professional people and ordinary non-professional people. Before recommending to a court that a child should be adopted, local authorities and agencies take advice from their adoption panels. If a child is being adopted by a step-parent or other family member, the local authority provides a report for the assistance of the court.

All reports to the court in adoption proceedings will contain information about the history and family background of the child who is to be adopted, with similar details about the prospective adopters. Medical reports must be provided by prospective adopters, because anyone who is suffering from a condition which is life-threatening or disabling, in a way which will make it difficult to care for a child, is unlikely to be considered as an adopter. The information provided to the court is obviously completely confidential, which can mean that if you are adopting a child you could find that there will be some reports which you will not be allowed to see.

What Happens if the Natural Parent Does Not Consent?

The natural parents of the child must consent to the adoption. However, if they refuse to do so, the court can sometimes dispense with their consent. In some cases there is a real dispute about whether or not a particular child should be adopted.

CASE STUDY

> Marianne, who is an unmarried eighteen-year-old, gives birth to Louis. She decides that she can't give Louis the stability and material advantages that he could be given by adopters, so agrees that he should be placed by the local authority with Martin and Carole with a view to his being adopted by them. Before the matter comes to court for the adoption order to be made, Marianne changes her mind. Louis has been with Martin and Carole since shortly after his birth and they already love him as their own child. They are frantic with worry about losing him. The test for the court is whether Marianne's refusal to consent to the adoption is reasonable. In all the circumstances of Marianne's case, the court

decides that her refusal to consent is not reasonable. It can then go on to make the adoption order, dispensing with Marianne's consent.

CASE STUDY

Rachel and Joe are the divorced parents of Jesse, who is six years old. They separated when Jesse was three. Rachel has married again. Her new husband Bernard wants to adopt Jesse. But Joe does not agree that Jesse should be adopted. He does not see Jesse on a regular basis, but he has had contact on two or three occasions a year since he and Rachel separated. He sends Jesse birthday and Christmas presents. Sometimes he telephones him. Jesse does not remember living with his father but he does know who he is. In all the circumstances, the court decides that Joe's consent to Jesse's adoption by Bernard is not being unreasonably withheld. Consequently, the adoption order is refused.

Once again, remember that every case is decided by the court on its own facts, and no two cases have identical facts. These case studies are merely examples of what might be decided.

The consent of a natural parent to a proposed adoption might also be withheld in a case where the child has been removed from home and taken into care because there were serious concerns about risks to the child in the home situation. The first objective of local authorities and courts must be to keep children in their birth families whenever it is possible to do so. Social services have a legal duty to give families support in an effort to help them stay together.

But there are still many cases where massive support has been offered by social services and has failed to improve the home situation sufficiently for it to be in a child's interests to remain with or return home to birth parents. Or the child may have been so seriously abused, emotionally, physically or sexually, that the risk of a return home cannot possibly be taken. In cases like that the local authority may ask the court to place the child for adoption. Often the parents will not consent to this.

Where a parent refuses consent the court has to look at the situation from the point of view of a "reasonable parent". Would a reasonable parent, knowing all the facts and acting in the best interests of the child, have given consent to the adoption? If so, the court can say that the parental consent is being unreasonably withheld. This means that the adoption order can be made even though the natural parent does not consent.

Does the Child Have a Say?

The government is contemplating changes in the existing law relating to adoption and has recently published a White Paper setting out the proposals. In line with the thinking behind the Children Act, one of the first proposals made in the White Paper is that a child aged twelve or more must agree before an adoption order can be made in respect of that child. A further proposal is that the child should have a right to be a party to the adoption proceedings and to be legally represented so that his or her views can be given to the court.

Can an Adopted Child Contact the Birth Family?

In recent years there has been an increasing tendency for "open adoption" orders to be made. These orders have been called open adoption orders because the link with the child's birth family has not been completely cut. Obviously, the older the child, the more memories of his or her birth family there will be. In many cases, even where a child has been seriously neglected or abused in the natural family, there will still be a strong emotional link with a parent or other relative, such as a grandparent.

In some of those cases, the court has taken the view that it is in the interests of that child to preserve the link with that family member, even after an adoption order has been made. The link could be through contact by letters or birthday and Christmas cards or gifts. It might even take the form of face-to-face contact once or twice a year.

There are cases where contact will be much more significant. It may be decided by the court, for example, that ongoing contact should take place several times a year between brothers or sisters who have been separately adopted. The test will always be what would be in the best interests of the children concerned, but it is not unknown for the court to consider that contact between siblings is of overriding importance in a case where the children have close emotional links.

This can pose considerable problems. Not every couple wishing to adopt a child is prepared for that child's natural family to have ongoing contact with the child, however infrequent that contact may be. While prospective adopters are sometimes prepared to agree to and even encourage inter-sibling contact, the suggestion of contact with a natural parent or grandparent can be less easy to take. This in turn means that finding a suitable match of prospective adopters for the child can be trickier for the adoption agency.

Nor are experts by any means in agreement about the benefits of open adoption. Some firmly believe that ongoing contact with the birth family, no matter how minimal, can undermine the child's ability to form a positive new relationship with the adopting family and so endanger the success of the whole enterprise.

In considering this dilemma, the government takes the view that the most important objective is to support the new family relationship. Where the birth parents wish to retain direct contact, free consent to that must be given by the child and the new family. However, where the adoptive parents are against the contact, their view should prevail. The White Paper does recognise, nevertheless, that in the case of older children who have been adopted out of families with whom they have formed a close bond the issues need particularly careful judgment and the child's view will become correspondingly significant.

The proposal is that courts and adoption agencies should assess the most suitable arrangements for contact between the birth family and a child *after* the adoption. Presumably, the intention is that no court should make an order freeing a child for adoption with a condition attached that there should be ongoing contact with the birth family in some form or another. Only after the adoption order has been made will the court be able to look at the question of ongoing contact.

Again, it can be foreseen that problems could arise. The adoption order is irrevocable, but there will be some adoptive parents who will not agree to adopt if they think contact is to be ongoing. So, with great respect to the government's proposals, how *can* the question of ongoing contact be left until after the adoption?

Telling the child

The White Paper rightly emphasises the need to make adopted children aware "at a suitable stage" that they have been adopted. In the past, it sometimes happened that a child would grow to adolescence, even adulthood, without becoming aware that he or she had been adopted by the parents who had always been regarded as birth parents.

The adoptive parents would probably have withheld the facts from their child from the best possible motives, perhaps because they could not bring themselves to break the news, perhaps even thinking that the child need never discover the truth. But so far as the child was concerned the discovery that he or she had in fact been adopted could come as the most profound shock, almost invariably triggering off an emotional reaction which might result in deep psychological effects. The saddest cases of all would be where a child first heard of his adoption through the taunt of another child.

Few adoptive parents nowadays have not been counselled as to the way in which they should approach the question of the adoption with their child. In the case of an adoption of a baby or toddler, undoubtedly the best and easiest way is to bring the child up with the realisation that he or she has been adopted. Telling a child the story of how he or she was specially chosen by the parents is a positive line of approach.

One wise and experienced family judge, himself a grandfather, always instructed adoptive parents that their child was to have two birthday celebrations – one on the birth date and one on the date when the adoption order had been made. That immediately made adoption something which other children would wish had happened to them too. Needless to say, children brought to him for an adoption order who were old enough to understand the recommendation were always very much in favour of it!

Older children who are adopted will usually have a "life story book" which has been prepared by a social worker. The book will contain photographs and information about their birth families and a history of how the child came to be adopted.

Finding the birth family

Where there is no ongoing contact with the birth family, the time may come when an adopted child wants to know more about it. Equally, birth parents may wish to establish later contact. Great care must be taken to preserve confidentiality in these situations because, for example, the birth mother may have made a new life for herself and never told her husband or children about the adopted child.

To find out information about a child's birth family, you should approach the Adoption Contact Register (address at the end of the chapter) which is organised by the Office of Population Censuses and Surveys. This enables birth parents, and adopted children once they reach the age of eighteen, to apply for the information necessary to make contact with one another. Such information is provided only when both parents and child agree that it should be.

Although such curiosity is natural, there are situations where a child or his or her natural parents will not wish to be contacted. The child may feel such loyalty to the adoptive parents that he/she does not wish to contact the birth parents. Or a mother, who had her child by a relationship prior to her marriage of which her husband knows nothing, may be fearful of the impact on her life were the child to make contact.

It is right that people in vulnerable positions should have their right to privacy protected. In order to afford such protection, it is proposed that in future the birth parents and other relatives will be able to record on the Register that they do not wish to be contacted. The adopted child will have the same right. Where such an indication has been given, no information will be obtainable from the Register.

Adoption agencies will have three main functions concerning contact:

(1) To make arrangements to keep open the possibility of voluntary contact after adoption.
(2) To consult birth parents about whether they wish to be kept informed about their child's progress and to counsel them as to the benefits and disadvantages.
(3) To counsel the adoptive parents and ascertain their wishes and those of the child.

Adopted children will continue to have the right to apply to the Registrar General once they reach the age of eighteen for the information they need to obtain a copy of their birth certificates. Full birth certificates normally contain the names and addresses of the natural parents at the date of birth.

Who Should Adopt?

From time to time there are worrying stories in the media about the approach to adoption taken by some local authorities. A toddler may be uprooted from the only family he/she has ever consciously known simply because the child and the family are not an ethnic match. It is on such occasions that the suspicion arises that a doctrinaire approach is overriding considerations of what may be in the best interests of a particular child.

CASE STUDY

> Ahmed's parents, originally from Pakistan, were living in London when he was born. Ahmed was taken into care by the local authority shortly after his birth due to serious concerns about the risk to him in the care of his natural parents. He was placed with foster parents, Syl and Bert, who were English. The local authority had intended that this should be a short-term placement, since it was their policy that children should be placed in families which were an ethnic "match" for the child. In fact, no alternative placement was found and Ahmed remained with Syl and Bert until he was three years old. At that stage the local authority decided to ask the court for permission to look for adoptive parents for him. Although Syl and Bert had by this time become so fond of Ahmed that they wished to put themselves forward to be considered as his adopters, the local authority made it clear that, because of their ethnic match policy, they would not consider the foster parents as possible adopters. Syl and Bert challenged this decision in court and it was decided that Ahmed, having known no other family, looked upon them as his parents. In his interests, Syl and Bert should be allowed to adopt him.

Nobody would argue against the view that children should be matched as closely as possible with prospective adoptive families. It has always been a requirement of the law that those responsible for adoption should have regard, so far as practicable, to any wishes of a child's parents or guardians in regard to the religious upbringing of the child. It is proposed that this provision should be maintained in the new legislation, and that the wishes of the child, if old enough to have an opinion, will also be taken into account.

The White Paper points out that the 1976 Act contained no reference to ethnicity or culture. However, in recent years these considerations have usually been taken into account. It is proposed that there will be a broad requirement to consider ethnicity and culture in the future when trying to match a child with an adoptive family.

However, the White Paper considers that in some cases it has been clear that those who are assessing prospective adopters may have placed too much importance on ethnicity or culture and not made a balanced overall judgment of the suitability of the parents for that reason. Although ethnicity and culture are factors to be considered they should not necessarily be more influential than any other factors.

It is considered that there has been no research which conclusively demonstrates that children adopted by people of a different ethnic group will necessarily encounter problems of identity or prejudice later in life. The White Paper indicates that in relation to ethnicity and culture any preferences expressed by the birth parents or the child, if old enough, should be given weight among other factors covering all the characteristics, circumstances and needs of the child. The most important assessment should be the ability of the proposed adopters to help and support that child through all the challenges he or she will face in life, rather than overstress any risk of difficulty which might arise from ethnic background.

Single people and unmarried couples

You do not have to be a married couple to apply for adoption – but it helps. The key principle, as set out in the White Paper, is to give the adopted child as far as possible the same prospect as other children have of successful development into adulthood through a stable and enduring relationship with two parents. Married couples are preferred because they have made a public commitment to permanency in their relationship, which is considered to give a better prospect of stability for the child.

However, it is acknowledged that some children, often with special needs, are successfully adopted by unmarried women, divorced women or young widows. There are other cases in which adoption by a single person may be the best option for a child – for example, in the case of a widowed stepfather with whom the child lived before the mother's death. The White Paper does not envisage that unmarried couples should be able to apply for adoption.

Age

Age has sometimes been a factor which ruled against prospective adopters who were otherwise suitable. It is important for local authorities and agencies to check that people wishing to adopt have a reasonable expectation of continuing health and vigour to care for a child until that child is grown up.

Age is clearly relevant in this assessment, but the White Paper emphasises that there should be some flexibility. Parents in their forties may well have much to bring to the care and upbringing of adopted children.

The White Paper states: "Throughout the assessment process prospective adopters are entitled to expect to be treated with courtesy and sensitivity; that the assessment made will be fair and objective; and that it will not be distorted by dogmatic attitudes on such matters as the suitability of trans-racial adoptions or the suitable age for adoptive parents."

It is intended that a new complaints procedure will be introduced to ensure that these standards are kept up.

Overseas Adoption

Increased and dramatic media coverage of disaster areas in Third World countries has brought the haunting little faces of starving or abandoned children right into our living-rooms. The collapse of communist regimes in Eastern Europe, with the consequent media focus on the plight of children in war-ravaged areas, has sparked off fresh concern. Many couples have offered homes to children from overseas, only to be confronted by the huge legal obstacles which have to be surmounted in the case of overseas adoption. The White Paper makes proposals which it is hoped will clarify and simplify the procedures for adopting children from overseas in this country.

If you are interested in adopting a child from overseas you should contact British Agencies for Adoption and Fostering (BAAF), address given at the end of this chapter.

Useful Addresses

National Organisation for the Counselling of Adoptees and Parents (NORCAP),
3 New High Street,
Headington,
Oxford OX3 7AJ
Tel: 0865 750554

British Agencies for Adoption and Fostering (BAAF),
11 Southwark Street,
London SE1
Tel: 071 407 8800
(for information on all aspects of adoption including overseas adoption)

General Register Office (Births, Marriages, Deaths),
St Catherine's House,
10 Kingsway,
London WC2B 6JP

NCH Action for Children,
85 Highbury Park,
London N5 1UD
Tel: 071 226 2033

Catholic Children's Society (Crusade of Rescue),
73 St Charles Square,
London W10 6EJ
Tel: 081 969 5305

Norwood Child Care (service for Jewish children and their families),
221 Golders Green Road,
London NW11
Tel: 081 458 3262

The Registrar General,
Adopted Children's Register,
Titchfield,
Fareham,
Hants PO15 5RR
or New Register House,
Edinburgh EH1 3YT
or Oxford House,
49–55 Chichester Street,
Belfast BT1 4HL

Post-Adoption Centre,
8 Torriano Mews,
Torriano Avenue,
London NW5 2RZ
Tel: 071 284 0555

Natural Parents' Support Group (NPSG),
10 Alandale Crescent,
Garforth,
Leeds LS25 1DH
Tel: 0532 868489

Parent to Parent Information Adoption Services (PPIAS),
Lower Boddington,
Daventry,
Northamptonshire NN11 6YB
Tel: 0327 60295

Parents' Aid (for those whose children are taken into care or who
are adopted without the parents's consent),
Parents' Aid Office,
Hare Street Family Centre,
Harbuts Road,
Harlow
Essex CM19 4FU
Tel: 0279 452166

Parents for Children (older and hard-to-place children),
41 Southgate Road,
London N1 3JP

11

FOSTERING

If you are thinking of becoming a foster carer it is as well to remember that you need rather special qualities. A foster parent is someone who becomes a parent, but only for a period of time. You have to care for a child just as though the child were your own, but you must always keep in mind that he/she is not. This can be a lot harder than it sounds. Through caring for a child you are quite likely to become attached and feel as though you were the parent. Fostering is a temporary arrangement – even though it may be long-term – therefore foster carers have to be on their guard against making too much of an emotional commitment to the children in their care.

There are all sorts of reasons why a child might need foster care – from the child whose mother has had to go into hospital for a short time to the child whose parents are, for some reason, unable to carry on as parents, and who needs a long-term substitute family. Another common situation is where a child is suffering from some kind of permanent disability and needs foster care for short periods in order to give his or her own parents a break. Depending on the circumstances you can care for a foster child for a period which can be as brief as a couple of days or last for years, even throughout the whole of his or her childhood.

Sometimes there are close relatives who can care for children in these situations, but of course this is not always possible.

The relatives may live a long way away from the parents, or have jobs or other commitments which make it impossible for them to offer assistance. However, where members of the extended family can help, it is possible for them to become approved foster carers, and they can then receive financial and other kinds of support from the local authority.

Another aspect of being a foster carer which requires careful thought is that children in foster care will need to see as much of their natural parents as possible. This will often mean that the natural parents will be visiting and/or making telephone calls to the foster home on a regular basis. So obviously, if you are going to be a foster carer, you will have to be prepared to co-operate with natural parents to ensure that the children keep their ties with them.

Private Fostering

If you are going to look after a child aged under sixteen for more than twenty-eight days, and you are not a relation or legal guardian of that child, you will be acting as the child's foster carer. It makes no difference whether or not you are being paid any money for looking after the child. So if you are planning to look after someone else's child for more than twenty-eight days you *must* notify your local authority social services department.

You should notify the social services department not less than six weeks and not more than thirteen weeks before the date when you will be taking over the care of the child. The parents, the proposed foster carers, and anyone else who has been involved in making the arrangements, all have a legal duty to inform social services about the plan.

Of course, a situation could arise where you are asked to look after a child for more than twenty-eight days in some emergency and it would not be possible for you to give six weeks' notice. The child's parents might have been injured in a road accident, for example. In an emergency like that the local authority must be informed within forty-eight hours.

The local authority can forbid someone to foster. It can also make conditions about, for example, the number of children in a foster home, or the ages or sexes of the children being fostered. If social workers consider that a home is unsuitable for any reason, they can remove a child who is being fostered privately. When children are being privately fostered they are visited regularly by a social worker who makes sure that they are being properly cared for.

Local Authority Fostering

There are two types of situation in which local authorities will foster children in England and Wales:

1 When parents are unable to look after a child themselves for any reason, such as lack of housing, illness or other family problems, they can ask their local authority for help. The social workers will find a temporary foster home for the child, and the parents will be able to take their child back home whenever they wish to do so. If the foster placement has been for any length of time, it is usual for the return to the parents to be planned together by the parents, the foster carers, the children's social worker, and the child himself or herself, if old enough. This means that the move can be made with as little disruption to the children as possible.

2 If a child is being neglected or ill-treated in some way in his or her own home, the local authority must investigate and must take the case to court, if that is the only way to protect the child from significant harm. If the court is satisfied that the child is suffering or is likely to suffer significant harm in the home, and can only be protected by an order, it makes an order which places the child in the care of the local authority. When a care order has been made the natural parents will not be able to remove the child from care unless the local authority agrees or the court makes another order.

The rules

There have to be very strict rules about any fostering placement. The local authority has to visit any proposed foster home, make enquiries about it and approve it before children can be placed there. After the child has been placed a social worker will visit at regular intervals to check that the child is happy and well cared for. A child has to have a medical check before moving into a foster home, and will have regular medical checks while in the foster home.

The local authority has to make a written agreement with the foster parents about such things as the arrangements for the child's health, what contact there is to be with the child's birth family, and what financial support is to be provided for the child. The local authority also has to give the foster carers written information about the child's background, health and mental and emotional development.

If you are going to be a foster carer you have to sign an agreement which promises that you will

(1) care for the child as though he or she were a member of your own family
(2) notify the local authority of any serious illness or other serious matter concerning the child
(3) comply with any arrangements made for social workers to visit your home
(4) notify the local authority of any change of address or any change in the people who live at your address
(5) allow the local authority to remove the child on request
(6) not use corporal punishment against the child and not disclose any confidential information.

What about payment?

If you are going to foster a child privately and you are going to be paid for doing so, you will be making your own arrangements with the birth parents about what the payments should be. When you foster a child who is being looked after by a local authority you will be paid an allowance for feeding, clothing and looking after the child. If you foster a child who needs special care, for example one with a mental or physical disability, you may be paid a special allowance which takes the additional responsibility into account. Local authorities do not all pay the same allowances for foster placements, so you would have to find out what the rates are in the particular area in which you are living.

What kind of people are chosen to be foster carers?

Many different kinds of people become foster carers. The main requirement is that they can give a child a loving and secure home. Some foster carers already have children of their own. Some are older people whose children are grown up. Some do not have any children of their own. You can foster one child or several at a time, you can specialise in babies, toddlers or teenagers. Foster carers have all sorts of jobs and all sorts of homes.

When social workers are trying to find a foster home for a particular child they will have in mind the kind of cultural background and religious beliefs in which the child has been brought up. They will try to match these as far as humanly possible in the foster home, so that the child will find much that is already familiar.

People become foster carers for all kinds of reasons. Maybe their friends have enjoyed being foster carers. They may have read articles about foster caring or seen TV programmes which attracted them. Or they may have replied to advertisements for foster carers in the media.

If you have had no previous experience of fostering, you will probably be put in touch with other foster carers so that you can discuss what it is like to foster a child before you actually have one placed with you. In many areas there are foster care associations which organise meetings for their members. You will always have the support of the social workers from your local authority who have responsibility for any child placed with you.

Ideally, fostering is meant to be a partnership, between the foster carers, the social workers, the birth parents and the child, if he or she is old enough to take part in decision-making. It is challenging and, as always when it comes to caring for children, hard work. But if you love children, want to help those in trouble, *and* can love and let go, it is a most rewarding occupation.

How Do You Begin?

If you are interested in becoming a foster parent, you can find out more about fostering from the social services department of your local authority. The number will be in the telephone directory. Just ring up and say that you are interested in finding out more about becoming a foster parent. You may be asked a few questions about yourself and your family over the telephone. After that, a social worker will probably visit you or invite you to come for a chat about what fostering involves. Obviously, it will be necessary for someone from social services to check your home to see what sort of accommodation you have to offer a child or children. Social services will want to know who lives in your home and will have to ask many other rather personal questions about your family life. You may be asked to provide the names of people who will provide you with a character reference.

Useful Addresses

The National Foster Care Association,
Leonard House,
5–7 Marshalsea Road,
London, SE1 1EP
Tel: 071–828 6266

British Agencies for Adoption and Fostering (BAAF),
11 Southwark Street,
London SE1
Tel: 071-407 8800

Catholic Children's Society (Crusade of Rescue),
73 St. Charles Square,
London W10 6EJ
Tel: 081-969 5305

Your local authority social services department (in telephone directory)

IV

Families in Crisis

12

CHILD ABUSE

It is no exaggeration to say that the most horrifying crimes committed in our society are those against children. We are revolted by such crimes principally because children are by definition innocent and defenceless. The younger the child the more the protection and love which ought to be given to him or her by adults. Children are naturally trusting and affectionate. A betrayal of that trust must be one of the hardest things in the world to forgive.

In recent years, when people hear it alleged that a child has been abused, they automatically seem to think of sexual abuse. This is not surprising, in view of the publicity which sexual abuse of children has received over the last decade or so.

But children can, of course, be abused in ways other than sexually. They can have harm inflicted upon them by physical abuse which has nothing to do with sexuality. Appalling cases where children are subjected to the most terrifyingly violent assaults are distressingly familar. Neglect of a child is another form of abuse and the "home alone" cases now regularly reported in the news are making people more aware of this. Cases of neglect do seem to be occurring with greater frequency than in the past. This may be due, as with other forms of child abuse, to the fact that increasing numbers of children are living in households where one of the parental figures, and particularly the father, is not the natural parent. It may be due to economic deprivation or unemployment, factors which can lead to feelings of depression and hopelessness and a lack of ability to cope with the demands of bringing up a family. It can simply be due to sheer ignorance of what are the basic minimum needs of a child.

A more subtle form of abuse, but one which can be as damaging as physical abuse, is emotional abuse. I will be returning to this topic later in the chapter.

Sexual Abuse

Children are sexually abused at all ages, even as babies. Abuse can happen to any child, boys or girls, rich or poor, and the abuser can be male or female. The abuser is frequently a member of the child's own family or a family friend.

Does sexual abuse of children occur more frequently now than in the past? Or is it that society is more vigilant and so more instances come to light? Or that there is more help available and more victims are prepared to speak up? Has the proliferation of pornographic material in relation to children in recent years had an effect on the unstable personalities of potential abusers? Does the publicity given to child abuse in the media have the effect of encouraging further abuses?

Experts argue interminably about these questions and no doubt will continue to do so. What is certain is that, even ten years ago, court cases in which allegations of child abuse were involved were comparative rarities. Now they have become depressingly common.

The Cleveland Report

At the time when it was being recognised that sexual abuse of children was much more common than had been imagined, there was an unfortunate backlash of over-reaction on the part of some social workers and medical practitioners.

While it might be understandable that professionals were anxious to remove children who were at real risk, the consequences of this over-reaction could be and often were extremely damaging to the children concerned.

Matters came to a head in 1987, when public concern was aroused by events which had taken place in Cleveland. In May and June of that year an unprecedented number of cases of sexual abuse of children had been diagnosed at the Middlesbrough General Hospital there, and many children had been summarily removed from their homes by social workers as a result.

Parents, nurses, the police, and MPs voiced their protests and acute anxiety about what was happening. The matter became one of public debate. In July, it was announced in Parliament that there would be a statutory enquiry into the matter.

The findings

The enquiry lasted for seventy-four days and the report was published in the summer of 1988. Evidence was given by parents, paediatricians, psychiatrists, social workers, police officers, MPs and other people with an interest in the matter.

Although it acknowledged that doctors and social workers had been motivated by the best of intentions, the enquiry came to the conclusion that things had gone very wrong in Cleveland in the spring of 1987. In a period of five months, two hospital doctors who had become interested in the question of sexual abuse of children had diagnosed abuse in 121 children from fifty-seven families.

Children had been referred to the doctors in various ways. Some were brought by social workers as a result of allegations or suspicions that they were being abused. Some were referred by general practitioners, health visitors or community medical officers. Some children who had attended at the outpatients department of the hospital with problems totally unconnected with sexual abuse were referred. In many cases, brothers and sisters or other children connected in some way with a child where abuse had been diagnosed were also referred to one of the doctors, who diagnosed that they too had been abused.

Most of those children were separated from their families and their homes. By the time the report was published most had in fact returned home. The enquiry report criticised the doctors for their over-confident approach and it criticised social services and the police. It came to the firm conclusion that the desperately unhappy experiences of many of the children concerned should not be allowed to occur again. To that end the report made certain recommendations.

The recommendations

The Cleveland Report emphasised the danger which can arise for professionals that, when looking to the welfare of children believed to be the victims of sexual abuse, the children themselves, as individuals, might be overlooked and be treated as an object of concern instead of as a person.

The report went on to make important recommendations, which should be followed in all cases where sexual abuse of children has been alleged. Unfortunately, years later, many of these recommendations are still not being followed, with damaging results for the children concerned and their families.

Parents

The recommendations so far as parents were concerned were as follows:

(a) That they should be treated in the same way as the family of any other child referred to social services. Sadly this does not always happen: in one case where an allegation of sexual abuse had been made, a social worker told the father that she could not bear to be in the same room as him.

(b) Parents should be informed and, where appropriate, consulted at each stage of the investigation by the professional dealing with the child, whether medical, police or social worker. Parents are entitled to know what is going on, and to be helped to understand the steps which are being taken.

(c) Social services should confirm all important decisions to parents in writing. Parents may not understand the implications of decisions made and they should have an opportunity to show the written decision to their lawyers.

(d) Parents should always be advised of their rights of appeal or complaint in relation to any decisions made about them or their children.

(e) Social services should always seek to provide support to the family during the investigation. Parents should not be left isolated and bewildered at this difficult time.

(f) Case conferences (where all the professionals involved – social workers, teachers, the GP and the police – meet to discuss the case) are held at regular intervals. Parents should be invited to attend for all or part of every conference unless, in the view of the chairman of the conference, their presence would prevent a full and proper consideration of the child's interests.

What happened in Cleveland was an extreme situation. But it has by no means been uncommon for professionals to over-react where sexual abuse is suspected.

False allegations

Since the problem of the sexual abuse of children came to public attention, there has been an extremely worrying development. In cases where parents have separated and the parent with care of the child does not wish the other parent to have contact, it has become all too easy to allege that the child is being sexually abused. This is particularly so in the case of very young children. Unfortunately, there is no doubt whatsoever that these false allegations are frequently made by parents. The parent making the allegation, usually the mother, almost invariably achieves the first aim of making the allegation, in that contact with the other parent is terminated or is only permitted under the supervision of some other adult.

Most local authorities, hard pressed by financial restraints, are neither willing nor able to provide such supervision for regular contact. The parent making the allegation will object to every supervisor suggested by the other parent, so that eventually the parent against whom the allegation has been made will either be compelled to pay for supervision by an independent social worker or not be allowed to see the child.

The damage done to a child by a false allegation like this can be incalculable. First there is the loss of the relationship with the falsely accused parent. Even if the allegation is eventually proved to be false, months will have passed while it was being investigated.

During that time any contact between parent and child will have taken place in the totally artificial environment of supervision. Investigations will be going on. The child may be interviewed by police officers and social workers, perhaps on more than one occasion. An intimate medical examination, extremely distressing to the child, may take place. There may be more than one physical examination. A psychiatrist or child psychologist may be asked to investigate. It is not uncommon for a young child to have several sessions with such experts.

It has to be said that the quality and expertise of the various professionals who interview children in these situations varies tremendously. The real experts are sensitive and objective. They do not approach the interviews with their minds already made up as to the truth of the allegations. They do not call the interviews "disclosure sessions", implying that they expect to obtain confirmation of already formed opinions. They do not ask the child questions which suggest the answers which fit in with their preconceptions.

Unfortunately for many children and many parents, there are professionals who fall far short of this standard. These are the social workers, doctors and child psychiatrists who accept without question allegations made by parents in situations where, with minimal investigation, it would be possible to discern the residual bitterness which remains over the breakdown of a relationship, and which should automatically put professionals on their guard.

The type of question asked by professionals overkeen to obtain "disclosure" is that of the social worker, producing an anatomically explicit male doll to a four-year-old. Helping the child to undress the doll, the social worker prompted, "He looks a little bit like Daddy, doesn't he?" The child examined the doll thoughtfully, then said, "Not really. My Daddy's got a moustache."

The American experience

False allegations of sexual abuse of children in the divorce context have become so widespread in America that the problem is now known as "SAID – sexual allegations in divorce". Such allegations, when made in the context of an acrimonious separation of the parents, are now treated with great reserve there. It should be obvious that caution ought to be exercised by professionals when the allegation that the child has been abused by the parent with contact initially comes from a separated parent with care of the child.

But the tragedy for some children and their parents is that it has taken some years for lawyers and other professionals to realise that allegations that a child is being sexually abused can be and are being made falsely in order to exclude a parent from the child's life.

When the allegation is false, not only does the child lose a parent, he or she also has to grow up in the care of a parent who promotes the belief that sexual abuse did take place, with all the resultant consequences to emotional stability in adolescence and adulthood which that belief entails. Parents who inflict that burden on their own children for their own selfish ends must bear a responsibility which is quite as heavy as that of a parent who has actually sexually abused a child.

Not all parents who make false allegations of abuse against the other parent are fully aware of what they are doing of course. For example, a mother who would really like to cut the father out of the child's life may misinterpret some perfectly innocent remark made by the child. She reports her suspicions to social services. Much will depend upon who speaks to the child. An over-zealous social worker with little real knowledge of sexually abused children can do irreparable damage by approaching discussion with the child in the wrong way. The social worker supports the mother's allegation and the mother, secretly delighted, convinces herself that it is not she who is curtailing the father's contact with the child but social services.

Young children are very suggestible. They can quickly learn, without understanding what they are being asked, that certain responses to questions from professionals are more welcome than others.

Emotional Abuse

The making of a false allegation that a child has been sexually abused is one form of emotional abuse of the child. Emotional abuse is not, of course, so easily detected as physical or sexual abuse, but it can certainly be as damaging to the child.

It is well known that sexual abusers also exert emotional abuse over their victims. Almost invariably the sexual abuse is accompanied by threats of what will happen to the child if the abuse is ever disclosed. These can range from threats that the child will be believed to be telling lies, to threats of violence and even murder. The child is frequently threatened that he or she will be taken into care and will not be allowed to live at home ever again, or that he or she will be responsible for breaking up the family.

Children who are being abused in any way by a parent very often still retain feelings of love for that parent. They are placed in an intolerable situation. They may not want to get the abusing parent into trouble. They may not even be aware that they are being abused. Many children, particularly young children, simply assume that what is happening to them happens to all children.

Above all, an abused child may desperately want to stay at home. He or she wants the abuse to stop, of course. But the threat of being taken into care may prevent any disclosure of what is happening. Sadly, lawyers and other professionals are all too familiar with cases where children who have been abused will withdraw the disclosures which they have made just because they want so much to return home.

Sometimes, when there has been abuse by a parent and that parent is prepared to acknowledge this and apologise to the child, it is possible that they may be reunited. Usually, this will mean that a period of months will be spent in family therapy to ensure that the child will be fully protected and feel safe before the return home can take place.

Children as weapons

Children can be emotionally abused in situations where there is no form of physical abuse. Parents with care who persistently make difficulties about the child seeing the other parent are emotionally abusing their children, whether they realise it or not.

Similarly, it is emotional abuse of a child for one parent to denigrate the other to the child. Most parents who allow themselves to criticise the child's other parent would be quite horrified to be told that they are abusing the child. But they are undoubtedly doing just that.

The important thing for parents to remember is that relationships may founder, but parenthood lasts for life. If they can only make themselves civil to one another for the sake of their children the benefits to the children will be huge. And they may even learn to like one another again.

What should you do if you suspect a child is being abused?

Most of us are reluctant to interfere in other people's lives, but children do need the protection of adults. If you have reason to believe that a child is being abused in some way you should contact the social services department of your local authority. Social workers will then check on the situation. You need not worry that your name will be disclosed.

Signs to look for if you think a child may be being abused

Schools, doctors and social workers sometimes notice that a child is behaving in a way which makes them suspect that he or she may be being abused. Abused children may behave in sexually precocious ways with other children or with adults. They can become withdrawn or tearful. They can exhibit fear of adults. There are sometimes, of course, physical signs such as otherwise unexplained soreness. Abused children often have nightmares. Someone who knows a child well, a family member, close friend of the family, or teacher, may notice that the child's behaviour has changed in a worrying way, when there is no apparent reason for the change.

If there is a court case will the child have to give evidence?

If a child has been sexually abused and the abuser is charged with a criminal offence, the child sometimes has to give evidence about it. It has been recognised that this can be a traumatic experience for any child. Arrangements are now usually made for the child to give evidence in a room away from the court, by video link, with some reassuring adult present, such as the police officer in the case.

In a civil case the child never has to give evidence. Any interview with the child, by a police officer, social worker or psychiatrist, designed to get the child to disclose details of the abuse, should be recorded on video, although it has to be said that this is not invariably done. The video can then be used in court proceedings.

Tragically, the sexual abuse of children appears to have become more common. Perhaps the only good result has been that facilities for helping abused children, through counselling and other therapy, are now widely available.

Useful Addresses

CRY-SIS Support Group (emotional support for parents of crying babies),
BM Cry-sis,
London WC1N 3XX
Tel: 071 404 5011

Parent Resource and Mother Support (PRAMS),
Churchgate House,
96 Churchgate,
Stockport,
Cheshire SK1 1YJ
Tel: 061 477 0606

Parents Against Injustice (PAIN) – (Support for wrongly-accused parents),
3 Riverside Business Park,
Stansted,
Essex CM24 8PL
Tel: 0279 647171

Survivors of Sexual Abuse,
Open Door Project,
Boundaries Road,
Feltham,
Middlesex
Tel: 081 890 4732

Childline
Tel: 0800 1111

National Society for Prevention of Cruelty to Children (NSPCC)
Tel: 071 825 2500

13

CHILD ABDUCTION

"Please, please, get my baby back for me!" How many times have you heard that desperate plea and seen the tear-streaked face of some frantic mother on a TV newscast or newspaper front page? Then there will be the photograph of the child who has been snatched by his or her estranged father. Of course, estranged mothers sometimes snatch children too. But these incidents are always a time of enormous stress, not only for the parent from whom the child has been snatched but also, of course, for the unfortunate child concerned.

Kidnapping, at one time, was a crime which was almost invariably committed by people who were strangers to the child, and motivated by an intention to blackmail the parents of the victim into paying huge sums of money for the child's return. It was more common in America than anywhere else and the kidnapped child would come from a very wealthy family.

The type of child-snatching with which we have become all too familiar over recent years is quite different. It usually happens when parents have separated, on acrimonious terms, and one parent (normally the father) does not accept that their child should live with the other. As the breakdown of parental relationships has become more common worldwide, international kidnapping – or child abduction as it is called legally – is happening more and more often.

CASE STUDY

Mervyn and Dee have been divorced. They were not able to agree with whom their seven-year-old twin girls, Lara and Petronella, should live. There was a court battle lasting two days, during which hurtful allegations were made on both sides. The court directed that the twins should live with Dee. Mervyn is a wealthy man. He likes his own way. The twins are on his passport. One day he simply turns up at the twins' school, tells the teacher that Dee has arranged that he should collect the girls, drives them to the airport and flies with them to a country which has no reciprocal arrangements with England about the enforcement of orders relating to children.

The court here orders Mervyn to return the children to Dee. He ignores the order. Dee is naturally extremely distressed. But Mervyn has forgotten one important thing. He still has a home, a business and bank accounts in this country. In a case like this the court can, and will, make an order that unless Mervyn obeys the order to return the children his assets will be confiscated. Mervyn cannot afford to lose the assets he has here, so he brings the twins back. On his return he is arrested and brought before the court. He ignored the court order and so he is in contempt of court. He is sent to prison for that offence.

In some cases a child may be wrongfully removed by one parent from the care of the other when both parents are still in this country. Any order then made by the court will be easier to enforce if the children have not been taken abroad. But of course it can happen that the parent applying for the return of the child does not know where the other parent has taken the child. In those circumstances the court can make a "seek and find" order, which instructs the tipstaff, a court officer, to make enquiries so that the child can be traced.

In cases like that the court may give leave for details about the child to be published in the media. This is exceptional, because the general rule is that no details about a child concerned in any court case may be published. But when other means of tracing a child have failed, the publication of descriptions and photographs of the missing child and the parent who has taken him or her may jog the memory of some member of the public, enabling them to be traced.

The court can also order anyone who might be able to give some information about the whereabouts of a missing child to come to court to be asked what they know. Grandparents, other relatives or close friends of the kidnapper who could possibly have information about the address to which the child has been taken, can be asked to attend court, for example.

What Do You Do if You Believe Your Child Has Been Abducted?

If you believe that your child has been kidnapped and that there is a real risk that the other parent may be planning to take the child out of the country, the police should be told immediately. If the child is under the age of sixteen, you do not have to have a court order forbidding his or her removal before contacting the police, but if you do have an order it must be shown to the police. The police will make contact with the immigration officers and warn them to keep a watch for the child and the parent at seaports and airports. If the child is over the age of sixteen, you must get a court order before the police can act. If the case is really urgent the court can make an order on the day you apply for it.

Before they do act, the police must satisfy themselves that the danger that the child will be taken out of the country is real and imminent.

If you have a court order forbidding the other parent to take the child abroad you can ask for a warning to be put on the child's birth certificate at St. Catherine's House (address p. 126). this means that if the other parent attempts to obtain a copy of the certificate in order to obtain a passport for the child, the authorities will warn your solicitor. The passport office should be informed of any order so that they can refuse to issue a passport for the child.

All too often, however, a child may have been spirited out of the country before anything can be done. With the increased ease of travel between one country and another, this problem was becoming so common that new laws had to be passed to deal with it during the 1980s.

When a Child Has Been Wrongfully Taken Abroad

The unlawful removal of children from one country to another had become such a problem that the situation had to be tackled on an international basis. There are two Conventions which provide for the speedy return of children who have been wrongfully removed from the country where they usually live and taken to another state which recognises one of the Conventions. This now applies to many countries including the USA, Australia, Canada, New Zealand, and most European countries.

This means that if you and your child normally live here, and your child is wrongfully removed to any country which recognises one of the Conventions, you can apply to the court here for an order that the child be returned. That order will be recognised by the other state.

CASE STUDY

Corinne and Del have been having problems in their marriage. Although they married in this country and their daughter Belle was born here, Corinne herself was born in Australia and all her family still live there. Corinne decides to take Belle with her to Australia. She knows that Del would never agree to this, so without telling Del, she books tickets and flies off with Belle to her family.

Corinne should not have taken Belle to Australia without the agreement of Belle's father Del, or an order of the court. Del can go to court here and obtain an order that Corinne bring Belle back to this country. The court in Australia will enforce that order.

Incidentally, Corinne has behaved rather foolishly. A mother who is genuinely feeling lonely and isolated because her marriage has broken up and all her family are living in another country can apply to the court for permission to take her child or children to live with her in the country where her family are living, even where the children have been born and brought up here and their father is English. The court will then make a full enquiry, through a court welfare officer, as to whether or not it would be in the best interests of the children to go with the mother or not. It is not at all unusual for the court to give a mother – or indeed a father – permission to take the children to live abroad in such a case.

Again, it must be emphasised that every case turns on its own facts. There have been cases where the court refused such applications because it considered that it would not be in the children's interests to have their contact with the parent in England cut off or limited by geographical distance. Corinne would certainly have prejudiced her chances of obtaining court permission to remove Belle permanently, by her behaviour in simply flying her off to Australia without even asking her father about it.

We must hope that eventually these Conventions will be recognised throughout the world. Tragically, where a child has been removed to a country where they are not recognised, there is nothing the courts here can do unless the parent who has snatched the child has assets here.

If the child is taken to a Convention country

A list of all the countries which belong to one or both of the two Conventions dealing with child abduction can be obtained from the Child Abduction Unit of the Lord Chancellor's Department (address at the end of this chapter). If the child has been taken to one of those countries, staff at the unit will take brief details over the telephone and will send you a questionnaire to complete. When you send back the completed questionnaire you must send with it:

a) copies of any court orders about the child which clearly show the court's seal;
b) photographs of the child and the person who has taken the child;
c) any other relevant information which might explain the circumstances of the removal or retention of the child or which may help in locating the child.

The Child Abduction Unit then makes a formal application for the return of the child, arranging for the details supplied on the completed questionnaire to be translated, if necessary. The formal application is sent, by airmail if appropriate, to the central authority of the country to which the child has been taken. The Unit will do all it can to speed matters up as far as humanly possible, but much will obviously depend upon the speed with which the other country deals with the case.

Under the Conventions no payment for legal proceedings in the country to which the child has been taken is normally required, although there are exceptions to this, particularly if the country concerned does not operate any legal aid system, as is the case, for example, with the USA. Again, the Child Abduction Unit will be able to supply information about likely costs, if any.

If the child is taken to a non-Convention country

If your child has been taken to a country which has not joined one of the Conventions, the situation is very much more complicated. If you cannot reach an amicable agreement with the other parent, or whoever has taken the child, you might have to instruct a lawyer in the country to which the child has been taken and institute legal proceedings in that country. The Consular Department of the Foreign and Commonwealth Office can give you a list of lawyers in any particular country who can correspond in English. Unfortunately, British consular officers in foreign countries cannot give legal advice or act as your legal representative.

Legal proceedings abroad may cost a great deal of money and British legal aid is not available for proceedings outside the country. There is a possibility that you might be able to get legal aid in the country to which the child has been taken, and any lawyer in that country should be able to advise about this. Another important point to remember is that foreign courts obviously apply their own laws. You might have a very good case in England, but the other parent could in fact have the law on his side in the country to which the child has been taken.

In some countries a mother does not have the same rights over a child as the father. Moreover, if you do not have the same social, cultural or religious background and it is your intention to bring the child back with you, these factors could well count against you in a foreign court. The lawyer of the country concerned will be able to advise you about all these matters.

Ways in which the Consular Department can help

The Consular Department may be able to help in the following ways, through British Embassies and Consulates abroad:

a)   by asking the local authorities for help in tracing your child;
b)   once the child has been found, trying to obtain a report on his or her welfare – this can only be provided with the consent of the other parent and at your own cost;
c)   if you decide to take proceedings, by asking the local court to deal with the case as quickly as possible;
d)   passing letters between you and the child (the other parent must consent);
e)   arranging for a room where you can spend time with the child privately (again the other parent must consent);
f)   informing the local authorities about any United Kingdom court orders which you might have obtained, provided the court agrees – these orders do not bind foreign courts but might be taken into consideration by them in reaching a decision.

Where a child is also a national of the country to which he or she has been taken (for example because the other parent is from that country) the authorities in that country are under no obligation to allow British consular staff to take any of the above steps.

If Your Child Has Been Abducted within the United Kingdom

Scotland and Northern Ireland have their own legal systems which are different from England and Wales. At one time these differences meant that a parent who had obtained a custody order for a child in England, for example, might be faced with the situation where the other parent took the child off to Scotland and obtained a custody order there. The English order might not be enforceable in Scotland and the Scottish order might not be enforceable in England.

The Family Law Act of 1986 put an end to these problems by providing that the courts for the part of the United Kingdom with which the child has the closest long-term connection are the courts where orders may be obtained about that child. Orders made about the child by those courts will be enforced throughout the United Kingdom.

If you want to enforce an order which has been made about your child in your favour you should apply to the court which made the order to register it in the court in which you wish to enforce it. The court will then send the papers to the appropriate court for registration.

Similar arrangements exist between the United Kingdom and the Isle of Man. The government departments and organisations which are listed at the end of the chapter are used to requests for urgent help or advice. You should not hesitate to contact them if your child has been abducted or if you believe there is a real risk of abduction.

Checklist

If you believe that there is a risk that the other parent might attempt to remove your child it is a good idea to keep handy as much of the following information as you may have:

a) About the child:
   full name, with date and place of birth
   passport number with date and place of issue
   physical description
b) About the other parent:
   full name and any other names by which parent has been known
   date and place of birth
   passport number with date and place of issue
   occupation
   probable date of departure
   flight information, if available
   details of ties with a foreign country – such as names, addresses and/or telephone numbers of family members, friends or business contacts
c) Copies of documents:
   any agreements or court orders about the child
   child's birth certificate
   up-to-date photographs of the child
   the most recent photographs you have of the other parent

Criminal Offences

It is a criminal offence for a person connected with a child to take or to send a child under the age of sixteen out of the United Kingdom without the "appropriate consent". A person connected with a child might be a parent, a guardian, or someone who has a residence order in respect of the child. If the child's parents were not married to one another at the date of the child's birth, a man who there are reasonable grounds to believe is the father is a person connected with the child.

If you have a residence order you are allowed, however, to remove the child or children from the United Kingdom for any period of less than one month, and you do not have to obtain the consent of anyone else to do so. This is just to ensure that a parent who has a residence order can take the child or children abroad for ordinary holidays without a lot of fuss.

The appropriate consent means the consent of the child's parents (if the father has parental responsibility), the guardian if there is one, and any person in whose favour there is a residence or custody order.

It is also a criminal offence, of course, for any other person, who is not connected with a child, to abduct the child.

Child abduction is a complicated subject. If at all possible it is best to consult a solicitor if you have a problem connected with a child who has been taken abroad or who may be taken abroad wrongfully.

Counselling, Advice and Support

Reunite (address at the end of the chapter) is a charitable organisation the main aims of which are to advise on the recovery of abducted children and to prevent child abduction occurring in the first place. It gives advice and practical assistance to parents and lawyers whether the child has been taken to a Convention or non-Convention country.

Reunite can supply information on national and international law, and can give you the names of lawyers both here and abroad who are experienced in child abduction and who speak English. It can also advise about raising money to fund efforts to recover a child and about how to get assistance in bringing a child back. Reunite also provides much-needed support for parents whose children have been abducted, by encouraging parents who have asked for advice to talk to other members of Reunite in their own area. They can also put a parent into contact with someone who has had experience of dealing with the country to which a child has been taken.

Useful Addresses

Child Abduction (a free booklet) is available from:
The Child Abduction Unit,
Official Solicitor's Department,
4th Floor,
81 Chancery Lane,
London WC2A 1DD
Tel: 071 911 7127

Reunite,
National Council for Abducted Children,
PO Box 4,
London WC1X 8XY
Tel: 071 404 8356

Foreign and Commonwealth Office Consular Department,
Clive House,
Petty France,
London SW1H 9HD
Tel: 071 270 3000

The United Kingdom Passport Agency,
Clive House,
Petty France,
London SW1H 9HD

Central Authority for Scotland,
Scottish Courts Administration,
26/27 Royal Terrace,
Edinburgh EH7 5AH
Tel: 031 556 0755

Central Authority for Northern Ireland,
Northern Ireland Court Service,
Legal Adviser's Division,
Windsor House,
9–15 Bedford Street,
Belfast
Tel: 0232 328594

Central Authority for the Isle of Man,
HM Attorney General for the Isle of Man,
Attorney General's Chambers,
Douglas,
Isle of Man
Tel: 0624 262262

14

DOMESTIC VIOLENCE

We seem to live in an increasingly violent society. Distressingly, we constantly see and hear reports of horrific violence suffered by women at the hands of men, appalling violence suffered by children at the hands of adults, mindless violence against elderly people and the mentally handicapped, racial violence, even violence committed in the name of religion.

There are those who believe that the level of violence has not really increased. They say that because violence is given more prominence in the media today we are given the impression that the problem is a new one, but that it was always there. They point to the Victorian society depicted by Charles Dickens and to the Yorkshire Ripper of modern times who inherited his nickname from Victorian Jack.

Other people believe that the media have to bear a heavy responsibility for the level of violence in the present day. It is true that it would be difficult if not impossible to spend an evening watching TV without having to view at least one scene of explicit violence. The producers of news bulletins no longer shrink from depicting the horrors of war or terrorism in the starkest possible detail. Fictional programme producers seem to believe that viewers are attracted by similarly explicit scenes.

The wide availability of video material depicting violence is another factor which some people think has contributed to an acceptance of and desire for more violence in daily life. It is argued that huge sums of money are spent on advertising in the media, in the belief that exposure to advertisements influences people to spend money on the advertised product. If the media can persuade consumers to buy advertised items, does not that suggest that a media diet of violence must have an inevitable effect?

The judge who tried the two young boys who murdered two-year-old Jamie Bulger is reported to have expressed concern about the possibility that those children had been copying what they had seen on video film. The debate will probably never be resolved. But one thing is quite certain: there is a high level of violence in our society and sadly much of that violence takes place in the home.

Battered Women

A man who inflicts violence on his partner is often thought to be uneducated and loutish. Unfortunately, this stereotype is very misleading. Many men guilty of domestic violence are professional men, men who would be taken for perfect gentlemen by friends and business colleagues.

The women who experience the violence are very often reluctant to seek help or to tell anyone else about it. A bruised eye will be explained away as an accident with an open cupboard door. A limp resulting from a kick will have been caused by a fall downstairs. General practitioners and hospital casualty units are all too familiar with such explanations.

For many outsiders it is very easy to say "why doesn't she just leave him, or do something about it?", but many victims are reluctant to seek help because they truly believe the man will change. He may have apologised, told her that he did not understand what had come over him, promised that it will never happen again. She wants to believe that, she probably loves him, so she hides the problem.

Another factor in the woman's desire to conceal the violence will often be that she blames herself for it. Many women are told by husbands and boyfriends who beat them up that they have asked for it, it is their fault. Even though they should know how untrue that is, they come to believe it.

Shame and pride lead some battered women to cover up what has been happening. It is so humiliating to experience physical violence that they lose confidence and lose their respect for themselves. Frequently, the abusing man will tell the woman that no one will believe her, and she almost comes to accept that.

It is a sad fact of life that children who have lived with violence between parental figures in the home very often grow into adulthood to repeat the pattern. The first few years of our lives are vitally important in the development of our future personalities. A child learns about life from his or her own direct experiences and those experiences inevitably shape his or her adult attitudes and behaviour.

The sons of wife-beaters often develop their own adult relationships in the same pattern. Violence has been imprinted upon their subconscious as an integral part of their concept of a man's relationship with a woman.

The same can be true for the victims. A seventeen-year-old girl was giving evidence in court about her relationship with an older man who habitually inflicted violence on her. She was an attractive and obviously intelligent young girl. She was asked why on earth she had put up with the beatings.

She seemed almost surprised by the question. "When I was little," she said, "my Dad always used to hit my Mum. So when my boyfriend hits me I know he loves me."

It would be wrong to assume that domestic violence invariably means that a woman suffers at the hands of a man. There can be few lawyers practising in the field of family law who have not encountered cases where women have made a habit of assaulting their husbands or boyfriends.

It is of course even more humiliating for a man to have to admit that he is suffering violence at the hands of a woman. These cases are relatively uncommon, principally because the man is usually more powerful and physically strong than the woman, so can defend himself. Also, a man who is being abused in this way will be even more ashamed and unlikely to want to admit it.

Changing attitude of the police

Not many years ago the majority of police officers would have been dismissive of any incidents where domestic violence was involved. Injuries which would have been severe enough to warrant a criminal prosecution, had they been inflicted between strangers, would be disregarded if inflicted by a husband on a wife. This attitude had more than a little to do with the view of the law that a wife was the possession of her husband, to do with as he wished.

It is only very recently indeed that the courts have accepted that it is possible for a woman to be raped by her husband. For hundreds of years the approach of the courts had been that the husband had an absolute right to sexual intercourse with his wife whenever he wanted it.

A leaflet which has recently been produced by the Metropolitan Police emphasises that domestic violence is a crime. Nobody has the right to assault you physically, sexually or emotionally. If you are being subjected to abuse, you should definitely call the police, who are committed to dealing with victims sympathetically and offering practical help and advice. In London alone sixty-two out of a total of sixty-nine police stations have domestic violence units where men and women officers who have received specialist training are able to give advice and assistance to victims of domestic violence. More and more of these specialist units are being set up all over the country, and all police officers now have instructions to treat domestic assaults as criminal offences, and to prosecute the offenders if appropriate.

Aims of domestic violence units

The objectives in setting up police domestic violence units are threefold:

(a) to provide a readily accessible service to victims and to assist them in making reasoned choices;
(b) to help co-ordinate social, voluntary and caring agencies, to pool ideas and to ensure consistency of approach to dealing with domestic violence;
(c) to raise the level of consciousness of police officers and of the public to the lonely and vulnerable plight of women subjected to violence in the home.

How can the police help?

First, a victim will be given the moral support of having someone who will listen sympathetically. A medical examination can be arranged if necessary. The victim will then be advised about the various options which are open to her.

If the police are satisfied that a crime has been committed the abuser can be charged with that crime and tried in a criminal court. Domestic violence can also be dealt with under the civil law without charging the abuser with a criminal offence.

(a) Criminal proceedings

The victim will have any criminal proceedings explained to her. If necessary a police officer from the unit might attend court with the victim to give her moral support. The officer would also keep her informed about what is happening with regard to court proceedings. For example, bail conditions might be imposed on a man who has assaulted his wife pending a full court hearing. Very often, those conditions would include a ban on his return home, for the protection of the wife. If the victim does not wish to take the matter to the criminal court, the domestic violence unit will keep a record of what has happened. If there is a further assault and the victim then decides that the matter must go to the criminal court, the record can help to show that there has been a pattern of violence.

(b) Civil law

Police officers will be able to refer victims to local solicitors who specialise in dealing with domestic violence in the civil courts. Anyone who has been subjected to violence by a partner can obtain an injunction from a civil court. The injunction is an order of the court. If it is disobeyed the perpetrator can go to prison.

CASE STUDY

> Marie has been assaulted by her husband Reg. She goes to the county court to ask for an order protecting her from further violence. Reg denies that he has assaulted Marie. The court does not need to hear evidence from either Marie or Reg. The case is dealt with by the judge asking Reg if he is willing, without admitting that he has assaulted Marie in the past, to promise that he will not do so in the future. Reg agrees to do this, as it is pointed out to him that no finding is being made against him and he is making no admission of violence. The judge then explains to Reg that his promise to the court will be in the form of an undertaking, which Reg has to sign. Reg's undertaking is that he will not "assault molest or interfere" with Marie. The judge will explain very carefully to Reg that if he breaks that promise he risks being sent to prison.

In many cases, the fact that a man has had to appear before the court and give such a promise has the effect of making him realise how shameful his behaviour has been.

CASE STUDY

> Lottie has been beaten up by her husband Max. She goes to the county court to get protection from him. Max denies that he

has assaulted Lottie and claims that the injuries from which she suffered were the result of a fall downstairs. Max refuses to give undertakings and wants a full hearing by the court. Both Lottie and Max give evidence and the judge accepts Lottie's evidence. The judge can then make various different orders, according to the gravity of the assault and the other circumstances of the case. One order which will certainly be made is that Max should not use violence or threaten to use violence against Lottie.

If the situation justifies it, the court can also make an order (called an 'Ouster' order) that Max should leave the matrimonial home, even if that property is owned by him in his sole name. Some orders specify that the abuser is not permitted to come within a certain distance of the home.

Serious cases

Where there is real concern for the safety of a victim of domestic violence, the police will discuss with her the possibility of moving in with some relative or friend. If there is no one suitable, or if the risk to her will be just as great if the perpetrator knows where she is likely to stay, the police will contact the local housing department to see whether bed and breakfast accommodation can be provided on an emergency basis. Women's Aid Refuges have an open door policy and are available on a twenty-four-hour basis, which means that every refuge must accept a woman in a crisis situation. They may then arrange alternative housing on the following day.

In cases where a victim is at grave risk or where children are being seriously affected, the civil court will sometimes make an order putting the perpetrator of the violence out of the home, even if it is his property. But even in the most urgent situations it will obviously take at least a few days before any court order can be obtained.

If This Is Happening to You

If you are the victim of domestic violence, please remember:

1 You are not alone. There are people who are willing to help.
2 You are not to blame. The perpetrator is the one with the problem.
3 You should contact the police. They will advise you of your options.
4 The police will let you make your own decisions.
5 The police will respect your confidentiality.

Useful Addresses

Women's Aid Federation (refuges for women and children),
PO Box 391,
Bristol BS99 7WS
Tel: 0272 633494
National Helpline: 0272 421392

AAA – Action Against Abuse of Women and Girls,
PO Box 124,
Chichester,
West Sussex PO10 3AZ

Alcoholics Anonymous,
PO Box 1,
Stonebow House,
Stonebow,
York YO1 2NJ

London Rape Crisis Centre,
PO Box 69,
London WC1X 9NJ
Tel: 071 837 1600

Men Overcoming Violence (MOVE – counselling and therapy)
33 Ivy Road
Bolton
BL1 6DH
Tel: 0204 848534
      061 434 7484

V

Practicalities

15

GOING TO COURT

Most people find going to court to give evidence in a case a fairly scary experience – and this includes lawyers. This is not really surprising. All the trappings of the situation, the judge sitting above everyone in his formal robes, the wigs and gowns of the lawyers, even the ushers in their black gowns, all combine to make the atmosphere very formal and forbidding. The layout of the court itself, familiar from film and TV sets, reinforces the solemnity. There may be members of the public there to watch the hearing, there may even be reporters from local or national papers, to make matters even worse.

It is your turn to be called to give your evidence. You have to make your way into the witness box, guided by the usher. You will be asked if you have a religion. If you are religious you will be given a copy of the Bible, the Koran or whatever is appropriate. The usher then hands you a card from which you read the words of an oath that you will tell the truth, the whole truth and nothing but the truth. Some people are so nervous that their tongues trip over the words. Others may have eyesight problems or may never have learned to read. If this happens the usher simply reads out the words of the oath which are repeated by the witness. If you have no religion you will be asked to affirm.

It is hardly to be wondered at that the minds of many witnesses go blank in those first few seconds. Most people can't help panicking a little. Am I telling the truth?

CASE STUDY

Connie was struggling to give evidence in support of her divorce petition based on the unreasonable behaviour of her husband. She managed to give her name, her address and the date of her marriage. Then her barrister asked her what the problems in the marriage had been. The wife had suffered several beatings from her husband. She would have to give details about some of the occasions. They were all set out in the particulars of her petition. But she was so nervous that she could remember none of them.

There was a long silence. The barrister tried to help with another question. The difficulty for the barrister was that no "leading question" can be asked in this situation. No question could be asked which suggested to the witness what the answer should be. The barrister could not ask whether the petitioner remembered the beating she had as a result of which she sustained a black eye and several bruises. "Do you remember the night of the 24th June?" Connie said she did. "What happened?" said the barrister encouragingly. Dead silence.

On this occasion, the judge did something rather unusual. He came down from the bench, walked round to the witness box, looked up at the tongue-tied petitioner and said, "You know what he did, madam. Your barrister knows what he did. But the silly old judge doesn't know, and you have to tell him."

That did the trick. But not every judge is quite so kind and compassionate, although most judges have sympathy with the feelings of witnesses who may be in court for the first time in their lives. They try to be as helpful as they can while keeping in mind that there are strict rules which have to be followed when evidence is given.

Thankfully, there is now no necessity for evidence to be given in the vast majority of divorce cases, where the whole matter can be dealt with on paper.

Although questions about children and financial matters relating to divorce are heard in court, the setting and atmosphere for such hearings are very much less formal than for defended divorce hearings. The judge and lawyers will not be wearing wigs and gowns. The hearings are in private, "in chambers" is the legal expression. There will be a notice on the door, "Court in Chambers", which means that no members of the public or reporters are permitted to be present in the court. Only the people directly concerned, who are parties to the proceedings, will be there, with their legal advisers. Other people may be called as witnesses, but they will not be in court except when they are giving evidence.

Occasionally, when matters about children are being heard, a judge will give permission for stepfathers and stepmothers to be present in court throughout the hearing, in addition to the natural parents. The decision whether or not to allow anyone who is not a party to be present in court is one for the judge alone.

Unmarried Partners

Disputes between unmarried partners about their children will also be heard in private. However, disputes about homes or other property between people who have not been married have to go to an open court hearing if the issues cannot be settled by agreement.

Before the Case

A lot of effort has gone into making courts more user-friendly recently. One result of this is that you will find that you can obtain a leaflet from most court buildings which will give you down-to-earth guidance on how your case will be dealt with. If you want to get hold of one of these leaflets you can ask for one at the court office between 10 a.m. and 4 p.m. on any week day. If you have any questions – and who hasn't! – a member of the court staff will try to help. Court staff usually wear badges giving their names. If you can't get to the court yourself for any reason you can telephone to ask any questions between 9 a.m. and 5 p.m. on any week day. You can also of course write to the court or send a fax. The address and telephone number of your county and magistrates' courts will be in your local telephone directory.

All documents relating to your case will have the name of the court at the top. There will also be a number in the top right-hand corner of the document. This is extremely important because court staff will always want to know the number of your case if you are asking any questions about it. Although court staff are not qualified to give legal advice, they will be able to supply names and addresses of local solicitors and advice agencies.

If you need special help

If you are disabled and need help you should inform someone at the court office before coming to court. All courts make provision for access for disabled people, although the older courts will not have been purpose-built with this in mind.

You might be anxious about coming face to face with other people who are involved in your case while waiting for the case to be called on. If you are, you can ask if it would be possible for you to wait in some other area. Again, whether this will be possible obviously depends upon the facilities which the court has, but staff will always try to help.

If you do suffer from some disability, it is sensible to inform court staff in advance because it may at least be possible for them to ensure that you have the minimum waiting time before your case is called into court. The court building will have toilets and public telephones. Some courts have a cafeteria. In others the Women's Voluntary Service (WVS) may provide tea and coffee. Some have drinks vending machines – although it has to be said from experience that these seem to break down with depressing regularity!

How to Cope without a Lawyer

The government has recently made cuts in the availability of legal aid (see Chapter 16). This has meant that many more people are having to represent themselves at court hearings in family cases. Daunting as it may be to have to give evidence in court, presenting your own case without a lawyer to help you can be even more worrying. But there are a few simple ideas which may help.

Preparation

1 Cases about children

Make sure that you know exactly what you are going to ask for or what you are going to say in response to what the other person in the case is asking for. In most cases you will be asked to attend court for what is called a directions appointment. At this appointment there may be an order, if it is a case about children, that statements should be filed by a certain date. A statement simply sets out the facts about your case. You should always put the number of the case at the top right-hand corner of your statement. The name of the court and the names of the parties in the case – you and the person on the other side – should also be put at the top of your statement. The paragraphs and pages of a statement should be numbered so that everyone in court can quickly find any part of the statement about which questions may be asked.

This is how a statement in a case about a child might begin:

Case No ......

IN THE ...... COURT

BETWEEN:

MARY X ...... Applicant

and

JOHN X ...... Respondent

1. I, Mary X ......, of ...... (address), make this statement in support of my application that ...... I am the mother of Adam X ......, who was born on .... The Respondent, John X ......, is his father.

After setting out who everyone is, you should continue setting out the facts of your case and what you are saying about them in numbered paragraphs.

At the end of your statement you say, in a final paragraph: I confirm that the contents of this statement are true to the best of my knowledge, information and belief and may be used in evidence.

Then you sign and date the statement, and take it to the court to be filed. The court will have given you a date by which the statements must be filed. If anyone else is going to give evidence on your side in the case, he or she should also make a statement in the same form.

You should send copies of all your statements to the person on the other side and, of course, keep copies for yourself. Cases about children are completely confidential, so you must not show any documents in the case to anyone who is not a party in the case or a legal adviser.

It almost goes without saying that you should never show a child any documents in a case about him or her. It is best, from the child's point of view, to involve him or her as little as possible in any dispute. Otherwise you put an unfair burden on the child, who will probably have very torn loyalties. The court welfare officer, or a guardian appointed to represent the child in the case, will be able to talk to the child about anything necessary in a neutral and sympathetic way.

2 Cases about money or property

If your case about family money or property is to be heard in the county court, directions will be given by the court about how the case is to proceed. The directions order might look like this:

IN THE ...... COUNTY COURT　　　　　　　　Case No ......

BETWEEN:

MARY X ...... Applicant

and

JOHN X ...... Respondent

DIRECTIONS

1. The following directions shall apply to this application.

There will then follow numbered paragraphs, giving dates by which each of the parties has to file affidavits of means and serve them on one another. An affidavit of means is a sworn document which sets out your income and your outgoings. You choose whether they are set out on a weekly, monthly or annual basis. But whichever you decide, please make sure that all the figures are on the basis you choose – it muddles everyone if you put weekly figures for some outgoings, monthly for others and annual figures for the rest!

An affidavit is headed in the same way as the Directions, and you set out the information in numbered paragraphs. You have to take it to a solicitor so that you can swear that the contents of the affidavit are true in his presence. The solicitor will charge a fee of £5, plus £2 for each exhibit to the affidavit. An exhibit is a document attached to your affidavit which you want to produce to the court – for example a bank statement or a wage slip.

The directions given by the court may include other matters. If there is a matrimonial home in dispute, for example, the court will direct that you and the other person must agree the value of the property. If you cannot agree, then each of you must obtain a valuation from an estate agent. At that stage, if the valuations are different, you ought to try to agree on a figure midway between the two. The alternative would be to bring the two estate agents to court to give evidence, and you would obviously have to pay them for their time which could be an unnecessary and expensive exercise.

Each case is different and this can only be the most general indication of what you can expect to have to do in a family dispute about money or property. Court staff will give you all the help they can, short of giving legal advice, if there is something which you do not understand. The directions order will always give the full address of the court.

On the day of the hearing

The court will have sent you a document giving the date and time at which your case will be heard. If for some reason that date and time are not convenient to you – for example, if you have a hospital appointment or are going to be away on holiday – make sure to get in touch with the court office immediately to let them know so that another date can be fixed. If anyone else is going to give evidence on your behalf, make sure that he or she knows about the date and can be there.

What to wear
There are no rules about what you should wear in court. However, judges are human beings. They, and any lawyers appearing in the case, have to observe certain rules about how they should dress, as a mark of respect for the court. So it does not create a good impression if someone turns up for a hearing looking scruffy or wearing, for example, a rather sexy and obviously unsuitable dress. Wear clothes in which you feel comfortable and reasonably smart.

How to address the court
In a magistrates' court the magistrates are called "sir" or "madam". District judges in county courts are also called "sir" or "madam". County court judges are called "your honour". High court judges are called "my lord" or "my lady". Do not worry unduly about what to call the judge, however. As long as you answer questions politely, the judge will not be concerned if you get the title wrong. Even lawyers get mixed up sometimes.

Timing
It is a help to arrive at court in good time especially if you are being represented by a barrister who may not have met you before. Although he or she will know all about your case because they will have been given full details by your solicitor, it is important to have a discussion before the case starts. Most courts open at 9.30 a.m.,

although there are some which do not open to the public until 10 a.m.
The hours will be displayed on a notice board outside the court or the
court staff can give you the information.

On your arrival

When you arrive tell the receptionist or the court usher, who will
be wearing a black gown and carrying a clipboard with a list of
cases. There will probably be more than one court in the building,
each having its own number. Find out under which court number
your case has been listed. If a solicitor or barrister is representing
you, he or she will want to have a discussion about aspects of the
case (called a conference) before the hearing. Your barrister is not
allowed to discuss the case with any of your witnesses, so may ask
them to stay outside the room where you are having your discussion,
or out of earshot if there is no room available. This is because there
must be no suggestion that your barrister has influenced what one
of the witnesses might say.

The hearing will never start before the time which has been given
to you. However, it is not at all certain that it will start on time. Often
you will find that several cases have been listed to start at the same
time. This is not as contrary as it sounds, because court staff have to
allow for the fact that settlements of disputes are often negotiated
outside the door of the court, so some of the cases may need time for
discussion. If one of the cases is settled by agreement, the hearing
before the judge will obviously be very short, just sufficient time
for the judge to be told what agreement has been reached and to
be invited to approve it.

When your case is called into court try not to feel too nervous,
especially if you have no lawyer to help you. The judge will tell you
when it is your turn to ask questions of other witnesses or to give
evidence yourself. Never interrupt when you have not been told it
is your turn to speak. Your turn will come and the judge will listen
to you with patience and attention.

Evidence

Your statements or affidavits are part of your evidence. You do not
need to tell the judge about anything which you have already included
in one of those documents because he or she will already have read
them. There may be other things which you would like to add when
you get into the witness box. The judge will allow you to do this.

Speak clearly and in a voice which is loud enough for everyone in court to hear what you are saying. Try not to go too fast, the judge will probably be trying to write everything down. A good tip is to watch the judge's pen while you give evidence. Pause until he catches up with you and stops writing.

If there are any documents which you wish the judge to read, you should have provided copies of them to the other side before the hearing. It is an excellent idea to make three photocopies of all documents which you are going to use in court, so that there will be a copy for the judge, a copy for the other side and a copy for you. If there are a large number of documents, put the copies in three bundles in the same order, with the same page numbers in each bundle. This will mean that everyone will be able to find any of the documents quickly. Make a written list of any questions which you want to ask each of the witnesses who will be giving evidence before you come to court. This helps to ensure that you do not forget anything.

You do not have to use legal language. Just say what you mean, in as few words as you can. If you do not understand something which is said, do not be afraid to say so and ask what it means.

If you are giving evidence yourself when the court adjourns (stops for lunch or overnight or any other break), remember that there is a strict rule that you are not allowed to discuss the case or your evidence with anyone during the period for which you are not in court. This includes your lawyer, so don't be surprised if he or she walks away if you try to speak outside court.

When you are asking questions

Trial scenes in films and TV programmes often give the impression that cross examination should be conducted in an aggressive and unpleasant manner. This could not be more unfortunate from the point of view of family cases.

Family judges will very speedily become irritated and displeased when anyone attempts to bully or intimidate a witness in a family case. It is much more sensible – and effective – to ask questions in a pleasant and friendly manner. Lawyers who specialise in family work rarely subject witnesses to the abrasive type of cross examination frequently seen in the criminal courts. If they attempt to do so, they are likely to find themselves being quickly rebuked by the judge.

Equally, when you are being cross examined, it is much more

effective to keep your replies polite – and as short as you can. Avoid asking questions in return – "How would you like to find your wife with another man?" is not a response which is going to find favour with the judge.

Keep as calm as you can when you are in court. It is difficult to sit quietly while someone is giving evidence which you might find hurtful and downright untruthful. The temptation to interrupt is sometimes very strong. But remember that judges are highly experienced in listening to evidence. Lies or exaggeration are quickly detected by them. Giving vent to your emotion will certainly not help and may indeed be to your disadvantage.

People rarely seem to realise that a judge is very much aware of everything which goes on in his court – one of the reasons why he or she usually sits in an elevated seat. Observing the reactions of parties listening to others giving evidence can be part of the judge's overall assessment of the case. So it is not just when you are in the witness box that your behaviour is important.

People who snigger or sneer when evidence is being given are not giving their own case the best chance possible. This is worth remembering whether you are representing yourself or being represented. Your lawyer will often be sitting in front of you, so will be unaware of how you may be reacting. But the judge will be very much aware of everything which is going on.

16

LEGAL COSTS

Taking a case to court is a very expensive business. This is one of the reasons for thinking very carefully indeed about whether you actually need to fight over children, money or the matrimonial home when your marriage or relationship breaks down. If it is at all possible to come to an agreement between yourselves about what should happen, you can save yourselves a great deal of expense, not to mention a considerable amount of emotional stress. This is where skilled mediation can help, and it costs very much less than employing lawyers.

But there are cases where there is no hope of agreement. So how do you go about finding a solicitor to advise you about your case? Not all firms of solicitors advise in family matters. The Solicitors' Family Law Association (address and telephone number at the end of the chapter) will be able to inform you of those who specialise in family cases in your area.

Another helpful source of information about local solicitors who specialise in family law will be your local Citizens Advice Bureau (address in telephone directory). Friends or relatives who have used a solicitor in their own family case might be able to recommend someone.

If You Are Paying Yourself

People are often worried about going to see a solicitor in case they find themselves facing an enormous bill straight away. But many solicitors in fact charge little or nothing for the first interview. Each solicitor has an hourly rate and will charge on the basis of the number of hours spent on a case. In the London area the minimum hourly charge would be about £80. The maximum could be several hundreds. A sensible first step when you make an appointment to see a solicitor is to find out what the hourly charge is going to be.

For a straightforward undefended divorce, with no disputes, £300 + VAT would be an average bill. But remember that every letter written and every telephone call made by your solicitor on your behalf will have to be charged for – it's rather like a taxi meter running all the time. Your solicitor should inform you of the likely costs before starting any work for you, and should also keep you up to date on how much your case is costing. You will probably be asked to pay some money on account at your first meeting, and then be asked to top that up with more payments on account as the case proceeds.

If your case becomes complicated or prolonged, if you are battling over money and the matrimonial home for example, the costs can run into thousands of pounds, particularly if there has to be a court hearing.

The first interview

An appointment with a solicitor can be made by telephone or by calling at the office. Explain briefly what your case is about when you make the appointment. That should ensure that you see the right person, because it is unlikely that everyone in the particular firm you have chosen will specialise in family law. Unless it is very urgent you should usually be offered an appointment within five working days. If it would be difficult for you to travel to the office, perhaps because you are disabled in some way, ask if it would be possible for someone to see you at home.

Because solicitors do have to charge by the hour, it makes sense to concentrate on making the most of the time as possible. A little preparation can be a great help. First be clear about the points you want to get across and the information which you need from the solicitor. A written list of the questions you want to ask and reminders of points you want to make is a good idea.

Collect together all the letters and other papers which you may have about the case so that you have them ready to bring to the interview.

At the interview the solicitor will ask you a lot of questions and make notes of your answers. He or she will be anxious to help. If you have questions, ask them. If the solicitor uses some legal word which is unfamiliar, ask what it means.

At the end of the meeting ask your solicitor to write to you confirming:

(a) that he or she has taken on the work;
(b) what advice you have been given;
(c) the name of the person in the firm who will be dealing with your case;
(d) the time everything is likely to take;
(e) when you will next hear from your solicitor;
(f) what the costs are likely to be in your case;
(g) whether the solicitor needs any more information from you;
(h) the name of the person in the firm to contact should you have any complaint about your solicitor's services

Keeping in touch

It is important to keep in regular contact with your solicitor. You should be consulted at every stage of the case about what is to happen. But do remember that it keeps the costs down if you avoid unnecessary telephone calls or correspondence with the solicitor. You should always ask when you may next expect to hear from the solicitor. If you do not hear anything by the promised date, you are entitled to ask why and to request a progress report.

Changing your solicitor

If you are paying your solicitor yourself, and you are unhappy about the way he is handling your case for some reason, you can change to another firm of solicitors at any time. It would be usual in those circumstances for your original solicitor to ask that all his fees be paid before he releases his file on the case to the new solicitor. If you have paid the full fees your original solicitor must hand over the file.

If you are legally aided you need permission from your legal aid area office to change solicitors. You have to explain why you wish to change. For example, you might have moved house and wish to change to a firm in your new locality.

If your firm of solicitors decides to transfer your case to someone else in the firm, they should tell you at once. If you are not happy with the change, you can take the case to a new solicitor (again with the permission of the legal aid area board if you are legally aided).

The National Consumer Council publish a helpful leaflet called *Getting the Best From Your Solicitor*, copies of which can be obtained from your local Citizens Advice Bureau or law centre (addresses in telephone directory).

Legal Aid

Solicitors who take legally aided cases usually display the legal aid logo prominently outside their offices. The Law Society (address and telephone number at the end of the chapter) will provide you with names of legal aid solicitors in your area. At your first appointment the solicitor has a duty to advise you if he or she thinks that you are eligible for legal aid. If that particular solicitor does not accept clients who are legally aided, he or she should still point out that you are entitled to it and would probably tell you the names of local firms who take legally aided cases.

Green form cases

If you earn less than £61 a week net and have a limited amount of capital, you are entitled to green form legal aid. In this type of legal aid you would be offered advice and assistance but not representation in court proceedings. The only exception to this is that green form legal aid will cover undefended divorce proceedings.

If you are the petitioner in the divorce your green form will cover three hours' free advice and assistance from your solicitor. This does not mean that you would actually spend three hours with the solicitor, as it includes time spent on, for example, letter writing, or steps taken in divorce proceedings. If you are the respondent in the divorce your green form only covers two hours of free advice and assistance.

Your disposable income will be calculated after deducting income tax, national insurance and allowances for any dependants you have. If, after those deductions, you have less than £61 a week, and have capital of less than £1,000 – £1,500 (according to the number of your dependants), then you will be eligible for green form legal aid. If you are in receipt of family credit, or you are on income support or you are receiving a disability allowance, you will be entitled to it.

If all this sounds complicated, remember that a solicitor can help you to work out whether or not you will be entitled. When calculating your capital assets in a divorce case, any capital assets which are in dispute between you and your spouse – for example, your matrimonial home, other possessions or money – will not be taken into account when assessing your entitlement to legal aid.

Legal aid certificate

This is the second type of legal aid. It covers representation wherever there are disputes in court about children or finances, but it will not cover undefended divorce proceedings. A legal aid certificate can be granted to cover a defended divorce, but this would be very unusual.

The financial limits for obtaining a legal aid certificate are more generous than those for getting legal aid under the green form scheme. Costs of housing and the repayment of debts can be taken into account when calculating net income. Again, your solicitor will be able to help you decide whether you would be entitled to a legal aid certificate. You may be asked to make a monthly payment, depending on your income.

If you have been granted a legal aid certificate you have a continuing obligation to tell the legal aid board about any change in your financial situation – if you get a rise in salary, a better-paid job or a win on the pools, for example. If you do not notify the board of such changes, your certificate could be discharged or revoked. If it is revoked you would have to pay back any costs which have already been met by legal aid.

Have you got a good case?

The financial test is not the only one which you have to pass in order to obtain legal aid. You also have to satisfy the legal aid board that you have reasonable grounds to take or to defend the proceedings. Sometimes your legal aid certificate could be limited to obtaining counsel's opinion on the merits. This simply means that your solicitor will ask a barrister who specialises in family law to give a written opinion that you are likely to succeed if the case goes ahead.

Your solicitor must also tell the legal aid board if he thinks you are being unreasonable about your case. If you were involved in a dispute about money and your spouse made an offer to settle which your solicitor believed could not be bettered as the result of a court hearing, it would then be the duty of the solicitor to inform the legal aid board and your legal aid certificate could be discharged.

Paying your legal aid back

If you recover or preserve – that is to say get or keep – any money or property (including the matrimonial home) as a result of your case, the legal aid board have to be repaid costs which have been paid by the legal aid fund, if the total which you get or keep is over £2,500. In matrimonial proceedings, if you do not get or keep more than £2,500, you do not have to repay the legal aid board.

In many cases the ex-wife or husband is given the matrimonial home as a result of the proceedings. There may be children living there. To avoid someone in that position having to sell their home in order to meet the debt for legal aid, it is possible to arrange for the debt to be a charge, like a mortgage, on the property. This means that the debt does not have to be paid until the property is sold. In some cases the court can direct that the charge should be transferred to another property when the matrimonial home is sold. Interest will be charged on the amount owing to the legal aid board until the debt is paid.

If the court has ordered that your ex must pay your costs, then your debt to the legal aid board will be reduced by the amount of costs paid under the order. But even if you get an order for costs you will usually find that the costs actually paid do not cover all the costs which have arisen. Correspondence between your solicitor and the legal aid board, for example, is not something for which the other side would be expected to pay under a costs order.

Useful Addresses

National Consumer's Council,
20 Grosvenor Gardens,
London
SW1W 0DH
Tel: 071 730 3469

Solicitors Family Law Association (SFLA),
PO Box 302,
Keston,
Kent BR2 6EZ
Tel: 0689 85022

Law Society,
113 Chancery Lane,
London WC2A 1PL
Tel: 071 242 1222

Legal Aid (for leaflets and enquiries),
Information Section,
85 Grays Inn Road,
London
WC1X 8AA

GLOSSARY

Abduction of child: wrongful removal of child.

Access order: now called a contact order.

Acknowledgment of service: document in which a respondent (and co-respondent if any) acknowledges that the petition has been received.

Adultery: sexual intercourse between a married person and someone of the opposite sex.

Affidavit: a written statement to be used in court the truth of which has been sworn or affirmed by the person making it.

Ancillary: incidental or attached to – ancillary relief describes the orders which the court can make about money or property which are incidental to divorce or judicial separation proceedings.

Answer: a defence to a petition by the other spouse (called the respondent).

Application: a document which sets out what the court is being asked to do.

Care and control: an order made before the Children Act 1989 which gave someone (usually a parent) the day-to-day responsibility for looking after a child; these orders have been replaced by residence orders.

Care order: an order committing a child to the care of a local authority.

Chambers: most cases about children or financial matters are heard in Chambers – no one is allowed in court unless directly concerned with the case.

Charge: like a mortgage on property – when the property is sold the holder of the charge (e.g. the other spouse or the legal aid fund) must be paid the amount of the charge.

Child of the family: any child of petitioner and respondent or any child they have treated as theirs (but not fostered children).

Child support: maintenance paid by parent with whom child does not live.

Child Support Agency (CSA): government agency set up for assessment, collection and enforcement of maintenance to be paid by "absent" (i.e. non-residential) parents.

Conciliation: does *not* mean reconciliation – an attempt to help divorcing or separating partners to reach agreements when there are arguments about children or money.

Consent order: a court order which sets out what has been agreed.

Contact: used to be called access – a contact order sets out periods and/or dates when someone (usually a parent) may visit a child, have the child to stay, write to or telephone the child.

Contempt of court: disobedience to an order of the court punishable by fine or imprisonment.

Co-respondent: the person with whom it is alleged that the respondent has committed adultery.

Costs: an order that one party pays all or some of the legal costs of the other.

Counsel: barrister.

Court welfare officer: appointed by court to investigate and report on a dispute about a child.

Cross decrees: where the petitioner obtains a decree on the petition and the respondent on the answer.

Cross petition: where the respondent claims that the marriage has broken down because of the petitioner's behaviour.

Custody: an order made before the Children Act 1989 giving one or both parents the right to make decisions about a child, now replaced by joint parental responsibility, residence and contact orders.

Decree absolute: the final order which dissolves the marriage.

Decree nisi: document certifying that the court is satisfied that there are grounds for a divorce – allows the petitioner to apply for decree absolute after six weeks.

Directions: orders made by the court about how the case is to proceed – e.g. for the filing of evidence.

Disclosure: providing information to the court and the other side.

Exhibit: a document which is referred to in and attached to a sworn affidavit.

Ex parte: an application made to a court without giving the other side notice.

Filing: leaving documents with the court office.

Green form: legal aid scheme for limited amount of advice and help.

Guardian: someone given parental responsibility for a child.

Guardian ad litem: someone appointed to act for a child in a court case.

Injunction: court order telling someone what to do or forbidding someone from doing something (e.g. where there has been domestic violence).

Legal aid: government assistance with legal costs.

Non-molestation: an injunction order forbidding someone to assault, pester, threaten or interfere with another person or persons.

Notice of application: court form on which an application is made setting out what is being asked for.

Ouster: injunction order which excludes someone from his or her home.

Parental responsibility: primarily the duties which a parent has to a child but also incorporating rights – a mother and the father married to her at date of conception or pregnancy have it automatically.

Penal notice: a warning on a court order that disobedience to it could mean committal to prison.

Petition: the document which asks the court for a decree of divorce or judicial separation.

Petitioner: the wife or husband who starts divorce proceedings by filing a petition.

Prohibited steps order: made under the Children Act to forbid a parent from doing something (e.g. taking the child abroad).

Questionnaire: list of questions asking for further information about financial matters.

Reciprocal enforcement: when two countries have agreed to enforce the orders made by one another's courts.

Recovered or preserved: money or property which has been gained or kept in the course of legal proceedings.

Relevant child: child of the family who is not yet sixteen at date of decree nisi or who is still in full-time education or training, or is disabled or dependent.

Reply: document filed by petitioner in response to answer and/or cross petition.

Reserved costs: where court postpones decision on costs until a later hearing of the case.

Residence order: made under the Children Act 1989 to direct where a child will live – only necessary where there is disagreement.

Respondent: the husband or wife who does not file the petition.

Service: giving copies of documents to the other side – some need to be served personally, others by post, some by you and some by the court – the court office will explain.

Special procedure: where the divorce is undefended (no answer filed by the respondent) there is normally no need to appear in court and a copy of the decree nisi is sent to husband and wife by the court.

Specific issue order: an order under the Children Act 1989 which decides some dispute about a child – e.g. where he or she should go to school.

Spouse: a husband or a wife.

Statement of arrangements: a form which has to be filed with a petition if there are any relevant children – it sets out the proposed arrangements for the children.

Statutory charge: the amount which has to be paid to the legal aid fund out of any money or property which has been recovered or preserved in the case.

Subpoena: an order requiring that someone comes to a court hearing.

Summons: an order that someone attends court at a specified time or date.

Undefended divorce: where the respondent does not oppose the divorce being granted.

Undertaking: a solemn promise to the court to do or not to do something; it has the same effect as an order, which means that a person giving an undertaking risks going to prison if he or she breaks the promise.

Without prejudice: anything said or written without prejudice during negotiations cannot be disclosed to the court if no agreement is reached.

INDEX